Assessing and Teaching Beginning Writers

Every Picture Tells a Story

David M. Matteson

Deborah K. Freeman

With a Foreword by Lesley Mandel Morrow, Ph.D.

Richard C. Owen Publishers, Inc.
Katonah, New York

All complete texts and excerpts are copyright and reprinted by permission. Grateful acknowledgment is given to the publishers and copyright owners for permission to reprint their materials. All possible efforts have been taken to trace holders of copyrighted material and secure permission for each selection. Complete publication information appears in the bibliography.

"Characteristics of Emergent Readers" in Chapter 3 from Developing Life-long Readers. © 1988 by Ministry of Education of New Zealand. Reprinted by permission.

"Characteristics of Emergent Writers" in Chapter 3 from Dancing with the Pen. © 1992 by Ministry of Education of New Zealand. Reprinted by permission.

"The Early Literacy Assessing and Teaching Continuum" in Chapter 4 © 2005 by Deborah K. Freeman and David M. Matteson.

"Monitoring Notes Form" © 2005 by Deborah K. Freeman and David M. Matteson.

The names of all the students in this book have been changed to respect their privacy.

Library of Congress Cataloging-in-Publication Data

Matteson, David M.
  Assessing and teaching beginning writers : every picture tells a story /
David M. Matteson, Deborah K. Freeman; with a Foreword by Lesley Mandel Morrow.
     p. cm.
  Summary: "The Early Literacy Continuum helps prekindergarten and
kindergarten teachers use observation of students' drawings, constructions,
and oral language to plan for and monitor development and meet district and
state early literacy objectives within a developmental framework"—Provided
by publisher.
  Includes bibliographical references and index.
  ISBN-13: 978-1-57274-741-8 (13-digit pbk.)
  ISBN-10: 1-57274-741-2 (10-digit pbk.)
  1. Language arts (Preschool)   2. Language arts (Kindergarten)   I. Freeman,
Deborah K.   II. Title.
  LB1140.5.L3M35   2005
  372.6—dc22

                                        2005008761

Richard C. Owen Publishers, Inc.
PO Box 585
Katonah, NY 10536
914-232-3903; 914-232-3977 fax
www.RCOwen.com

Acquisitions Editor: Darcy H. Bradley
Project Manager: Amy J. Finney / Phyllis Morrison

Printed in the United States of America
9   8   7   6   5   4   3   2

DEDICATION   To the teachers in my life—Ann Fontaine, Jan Duncan,
Marilyn Herzog Duncan, Margaret Mooney,
and especially my daughter Kerra
David

To the children of the past whose stories inspired
the creation of the continuum
and to Emily, Luke, and the children of the future
whose stories are yet to be told—
may they be listened to by wise and caring teachers
Debbie

Contents

Foreword

Research studies and syntheses conducted over the past decade have helped us understand the importance of young children's experiences with oral and written language. The preschool and kindergarten years are especially important for oral language development and initial experiences with reading and writing that link to later school achievement (Snow, Burns, and Griffin 1998; Morrow 2005; Whitehurst and Lonigan 1998).

In *Assessing and Teaching Beginning Writers: Every Picture Tells a Story* authors David Matteson and Deborah Freeman help teachers of young children focus on the intentional and appropriate planning of literacy instruction. I applaud the authors for dealing with this topic. What makes this book unique is that the authors have created an assessment tool called **The Early Literacy Continuum** for early childhood teachers to use in order to plan instruction. This approach to teaching literacy in the preschool and kindergarten setting makes the book extremely innovative. It is sound practice to teach based on what we know about the needs of children. The assessment continuum provides a way for teachers to identify what children need.

Quality early learning programs focus on language and literacy development and include standards for learning with outcomes described. These programs have teaching plans that are intentional and are developmentally appropriate for young children. This means that instruction is organized so it happens in small groups, in one-to-one teacher-child interactions, and in child-initiated experiences. Providing language and literacy experiences in these settings does not mean moving reading and writing instruction from the primary grades into the preschool or kindergarten, rather it means integrating appropriate literacy activities throughout the traditional curriculum in a thoughtful way (Dickinson 2002).

In this book the authors use vivid examples of teachers working with students. These vignettes demonstrate teaching that is based on assessment and learning that is on a continuum. I would further elaborate that the examples offer an appropriate range of literacy exposure for[1]:

- oral language experiences that focus on gestural expression, verbal expression, vocabulary development, building background knowledge and listening to others talk to understand (Dickinson, Cote, and Smith 1993)
- phonological awareness, that is, words are made up of individual sounds. Young children learn this in many forms of oral language experiences (Adams 1990; Adams 2001; Carroll, Snowling, Hulme, and Stevenson, 2003; Strickland and Schickedanz 2004)
- print conventions and book handling. This means that children have experiences learning that there is a front, back, top and bottom to books. They learn that there is a left to right sequence in books, and there is a difference between the print and pictures. There are experiences to learn letter names, to identify letters visually, and to learn letter sounds
- different types of text such as stories, informational books, poetry, folk tales, fables, and their own writing attempts help children to comprehend and develop an interest in books. The experience of reading to children is most valuable when accompanied by interactive discussions with adults and children to introduce new vocabulary and language structures. This conversation leads to understanding or comprehension of the story read (Morrow and Gambrell 2004; Storch and Whitehurst 2002; Bus, Van IJzendoorn, and Pellegrini 1995; Wells 1985)

[1]The National Early Literacy Panel (2004) studied research to identify abilities of children from birth through age five that predict later achievement in literacy. The abilities identified were: oral language development, phonological/phonemic awareness, alphabetic knowledge, print knowledge, and invented spelling. Researchers have also found that experiences with storybook reading, discussions about books, listening comprehension, and writing are crucial in early literacy development (Bus, Van IJzendoorn, and Pellegrini 1995; Wells 1985).

- experiences with writing attempts by scribbling, making letter-like forms, using invented spelling, and writing in a conventional manner. Writing teaches children about letters, sounds and the meaning of text (Schickedanz and Casbergue 2004).

The authors do more than discuss how to prepare programs for oral language, writing, comprehension, and knowledge about print; they talk about how to plan for instruction in these areas based upon assessing children's achievement. *Assessing and Teaching Beginning Writers: Every Picture Tells a Story* is packed with research and appropriate practice. It provides vignettes of real stories about student assessment and instruction. It deals with early literacy development in an interesting, caring, and innovative manner through the lens of assessment. It is a must read for all involved with teaching young children.

Lesley Mandel Morrow, Ph.D.
Rutgers University

References

Adams, Marilyn J. 1990. *Beginning to Read: Thinking and Learning about Print.* Cambridge, MA: MIT Press.

Adams, Marilyn J. 2001. "Alphabetic Anxiety and Explicit Systematic Phonics Instruction: A Cognitive Science Perspective." In *Handbook of Early Literacy Research.* Edited by Susan B. Neuman and David K. Dickinson. New York: Guilford Press.

Bus, Adriana G., Marinus H. Van IJzendoorn, and Anthony D. Pellegrini. 1995. "Joint Book Reading Makes for Success in Learning to Read: A Meta-analysis on Intergenerational Transmission of Literacy." *Review of Educational Research.* Volume 65, number 1, pp. 1-21.

Carroll, Julia M., Margaret J. Snowling, Charles Hulme, and Jim Stevenson. 2003. "The Development of Phonological Awareness in Preschool Children." *Developmental Psychology*. Volume 39, number 5, pp. 913-923.

Dickinson, David K. 2002. "Shifting Images of Developmentally Appropriate Practice as Seen Through Different Lenses." *Educational Researcher*. Volume 31, number 1, pp. 26-32.

Dickinson, David K., L. Cote, and M. W. Smith. 1993. "Learning Vocabulary in Preschool: Social and Discourse Contexts Affecting Vocabulary Growth." In *The Development of Literacy Through Social Interaction: New Directions in Child Development*. Edited by Colette Daiute. San Francisco, CA: Jossey-Bass.

Morrow, Lesley M. 2005. *Literacy Development in the Early years: Helping Children Read and Write,* 5th ed. Boston, MA: Allyn & Bacon.

Morrow, Lesley M. and Linda B. Gambrell. 2004. *Using Children's Literature in Preschool: Comprehending and Enjoying Books*. Newark, DE: International Reading Association.

National Early Literacy Panel Report. 2004. Washington, DC: National Institute for Literacy; National Family Literacy Association.

Schickedanz, Judith A. and Renee M. Casbergue. 2004. *Writing in Preschool: Learning to Orchestrate Meaning and Marks*. Newark, DE: International Reading Association.

Snow, Catherine, M. Susan Burns, and Peg Griffin. 1998. *Preventing Reading Difficulties in Young Children*. Washington, DC: National Academy Press.

Storch, Stacey A. and Grover J. Whitehurst. 2002. "Oral Language and Code-Related Precursors to Reading: Evidence From a Longitudinal Structural Model." *Developmental Psychology*. Volume 38, number 6, pp. 934-947.

Strickland, Dorothy and Judith A. Schickedanz. 2004. *Learning about Print in Preschool: Working with Letters, Words, and Beginning Links with Phonemic Awareness.* Newark, DE: International Reading Association.

Wells, Gordon. 1985. *The Meaning Makers.* Portsmouth, NH: Heinemann.

Whitehurst, Grover J. and Christopher J. Lonigan. 1998. "Child Development and Emergent Literacy." *Child Development.* Volume 69, number 3, pp. 848-872.

Preface

The audience for this book is early childhood educators and administrators who are interested in refining assessment and teaching practices and who see early childhood as fertile ground for young students to move along a literacy continuum. In particular prekindergarten and kindergarten teachers will find this book useful in understanding the developmental needs of beginning readers and writers and the instruction that supports them. First-grade teachers will also benefit from looking more closely at this developmental perspective for students who are not making satisfactory progress.

This book takes an in-depth look at an assessment and teaching tool which supports teachers in developing students' control of oral language and attention to picture detail through developmentally appropriate practices—both of which build a solid foundation for a child's later literacy experiences. In our work as teacher coaches in many prekindergarten and kindergarten classrooms, it was obvious that teachers had an understanding of literacy development but needed a tool with which to better focus their assessing, planning, and teaching while documenting student progress. As a result of these needs, the examination of many samples of young students' work, and extensive observation in classrooms, we developed **The Early Literacy Continuum.** The Early Literacy Continuum is a tool that will help teachers use observation of daily classroom activities in a systematic and ongoing way. The Early Literacy Continuum is also a convenient and effective way to structure district or state early literacy objectives within an organized and developmental framework. The continuum will aid curriculum developers as they align these objectives to the bigger picture of the entire district and as they work to meet those objectives in all areas of curriculum.

While the examples in this book mainly focus on the pictures or drawings made by the students, the continuum should be used to support the student's work in any area of the classroom. This might include a structure that a child builds at the block center, an object the child creates with modeling clay, or the natural conversations a child holds with others. Those experiences need the same attention to detail and oral language that is given to a picture and they can be assessed the same way. The more that the continuum is used within the different areas of the classroom, the more closely students will attend to detail within their work and develop the ability to converse about any of their work.

HOW THE CONTINUUM DEVELOPED

We developed the continuum as a tool to support the teachers with whom we worked. Before the development of this continuum, in one school, teachers were required to have every student write every day. Here is how one teacher described her attempt to meet that writing requirement: "I had all of my students write at one time. My assistant and I rushed from student to student so that we could get dictation from everyone. While attempting to take dictation I was dealing with a lot of off-task behavior as students waited for my assistant or me to take dictation about their writing and drawing. Students showed little or no progress in their writing and drawing or oral language development. Student work at the end of the year varied little from their work at the beginning. As most prekindergarten teachers do, I had always roved the class, taking anecdotal notes, but I never quite knew what I was looking for or how to apply the information I had gathered to my teaching. Have you ever known that things weren't right, but couldn't determine why?"

In an effort to support this teacher and others like her we began to examine the drawing and writing of young students. We noticed and began to categorize similarities. While some pictures included writing, it seemed that the picture held the meaning for the student. Some pictures were unidentifiable scribbles. Many drawings had some level of detail. Some were very detailed. Some students drew the same picture over and over but had a different story to go with each drawing. There was nothing to differentiate one picture from another. We explored what the students could tell about their pictures. As with the drawings, we found some commonalties in the levels of students' oral language as they talked about their pictures. Some students could not articulate what they had drawn. Others used one-word labels. Some changed their stories every time they told them. Others remained steadfast to the stories about their drawings. What became clear as we went through this process was that, by looking at the different levels in picture drawing and oral language development, we could see the next learning steps for each student.

Prekindergarten and kindergarten teachers needed a tool—a tool that would help them focus their anecdotal notes and ultimately their teaching. This is what teachers are saying about the Early Literacy Continuum. "As a preschool instructor of thirteen years, I have found the continuum to be the most practical, helpful, and constructive tool that I have used to date. It has been my guide as I have worked to focus my literacy instruction. The continuum has been an important contributor to my success as a preschool teacher." Another teacher stated, "The continuum is a great teaching tool. It maps out the different stages that children go through in their literacy development. The Teaching Objectives section has helped me more accurately identify where students are working and what their next learning steps are as they develop their writing skills. As a result, I am much more focused in my writing conferences with students. Because of the continuum, I have become a much better teacher." This final quote from an administrator sums up the power of the Early Literacy Continuum. "Finally a tool that helps my teachers focus their efforts on literacy activities that are meaningful to young children. The use of this continuum supports the true reason for writing: self-expression and the creation of meaning. This is a very empowering tool for teachers and their students alike."

HOW TO USE THIS BOOK

Each chapter begins with **Guiding Questions** for readers to think about in light of their own work in early childhood. These reflective questions are meant to inspire the reader to engage actively with the text as they put themselves into the detailed accounts of students and teachers at the important work of literacy assessment, teaching, and learning. The book is divided into two sections. Section I, Developing Theory About Early Literacy Experiences, consists of Chapters 1 to 3. This section explores the impact of theoretical perspectives on teaching and learning, the need for a stronger connection between prekindergarten/kindergarten and later school experiences, and the basis for early literacy instruction. Section II, Understanding How to Use the Early Literacy Continuum, comprises Chapters 4 to 8. This section begins by introducing and explaining the use of the continuum as an assessment tool. It gives rich examples of the continuum in action in order to clarify the distinct levels of student work and oral language. It also shows how to organize district or state teaching objectives to fit the broad developmental levels of the continuum. This section closes by looking at how two school districts in different states have used the continuum to organize for assessment and explicit instruction in early childhood classrooms.

ACKNOWLEDGMENTS

The development of this book would not have been possible without the input from many sources. Most importantly, our thanks and gratitude go to our colleague Kara Freeman, a prekindergarten teacher whose natural and self-reflective teaching had a tremendous impact on the development of this continuum. We express our thanks to educators at the Arlington Independent School District in Texas, in particular Dr. Jo McGovern, whose knowledge of young children has been an invaluable asset and who was first to recognize the value of the continuum. We also thank Bonnie Rhodes from Cartwright School District in Arizona for seeing the continuum as a strong component to the literacy initiative in her schools. Thanks also to the district's prekindergarten literacy coaches, Norma Veach and Maria Montoya, whose work greatly enhanced our understanding of the continuum's use. Thanks to Debbie Backus, Straz Strzalkowski, and Maureen Gurrini from Aurora Public Schools in Colorado, who see the potential of prekindergarten and are using the continuum to impact emergent learners and ultimately district test scores. Thanks to editor Darcy Bradley for her advice throughout the revision process. Thanks to Angela Matteson, whose classroom is always an inspiration and where many new ideas about the continuum have developed. Finally, our thanks go to Ken Freeman for serving as cook and chauffeur during our working sessions and for his patience during our hours of dialogue and writing.

SECTION I   DEVELOPING THEORY ABOUT EARLY LITERACY EXPERIENCES

Chapter 1

A Journey from Prekindergarten to Kindergarten

What teachers believe often dictates the assessment and instructional decisions they make. These decisions can assist, leave to chance, or impede how children learn, even during their earliest experiences in schooling. This chapter looks at the connection between prekindergarten and kindergarten and begins an exploration of literacy development.

GUIDING QUESTIONS

- What foundation do I need to provide for the children in my classroom for them to be successful as they progress through the grades?
- What connection should I make for these children between the prekindergarten and kindergarten experience and beyond?

MICHAEL'S STORY

Michael's Prekindergarten Experience

Michael began his school experience in a preschool at the age of four. Michael's prekindergarten experience placed a great deal of instructional value on social engagement. During the school year, Michael's mother, Janeen, had several occasions, both formal and informal, to meet with his teachers to discuss Michael's progress. Many of the conversations and written reports emphasized social behaviors such

- What foundation do I need to provide for the children in my classroom for them to be successful as they progress through the grades?

- What connection should I make for these children between the prekindergarten and kindergarten experience and beyond?

as, "...is very cooperative during Free Time." "...is a friend to many students in the classroom." "...behavior is improving during Group Time." Janeen recounted one informal meeting when she came to pick up Michael after school. The teacher, Mr. Bonner, took them to the side of the classroom to discuss Michael's "line behavior." Apparently Michael had been standing in line with the rest of his class as they waited their turns to use the bathroom. While waiting, several students fell into one another, causing them all to fall to the ground. When asked what had happened, many of the students accused Michael of pushing. Mr. Bonner wanted Janeen to know about this misbehavior and that he was working to help Michael learn to keep his hands to himself. During the ride home and for the next few days Michael insisted the bathroom incident had been an accident.

As Michael's school year progressed Janeen noticed that his recounts about the school day focused more and more on negative incidents. She tried to redirect the conversation by getting Michael to talk about what had gone well, but it was obvious from the way he talked that Michael was beginning to dislike school. Janeen was worried and, despite her efforts to communicate with his teachers and support Michael, very little changed during his preschool year.

Michael Begins Kindergarten

Before the start of the school year, Janeen expressed her concerns about Michael to Ms. Walker, who would be Michael's kindergarten teacher. Janeen was concerned that he didn't like school and that his overactive and boisterous behaviors reported in preschool would continue to be a problem in kindergarten. She was also concerned about his academic knowledge. The only information Janeen received in prekindergarten had been primarily about Michael's behavior. Ms. Walker assured her that he would be fine and not to worry.

Because of the conversation with Janeen prior to the start of school, it was a surprise to Ms. Walker that Michael was so quiet and self-controlled and exhibited none of the behavior that had been described. She noted that he was much more an "observer" than a "doer" in the classroom. Michael seemed somewhat reserved toward the other students and seldom participated during a lesson. Even when the teacher initiated a positive and encouraging interaction with him, he looked panic-stricken and seemed to have a hard time finding the words to answer the simplest of questions. Ms. Walker began to wonder about Michael's oral language. Even though Michael did not seem to know as much as his peers in terms of letter knowledge and sounds and writing a few words, it was his ability and willingness to communicate that seemed the more pressing issue to his teacher.

From the first day of kindergarten, everyone in Michael's class was expected to draw a quick sketch and write a story—no matter if the writing was random strings of letters or letter-like forms to go with their pictures. Ms. Walker's focus was to develop the students' understanding that not only pictures but words also hold meaning and that what is said can be written down and reread.

As the children drew and wrote, the teacher roved throughout the classroom with the intention to hear their stories and help them better articulate the story they want to tell. Though shy at first, Michael soon blossomed as his teacher encouraged him by showing an interest in what he had to say. Ms. Walker helped him uncover the "voice" in his story by asking questions and making comments about his

- What foundation do I need to provide for the children in my classroom for them to be successful as they progress through the grades?

- What connection should I make for these children between the prekindergarten and kindergarten experience and beyond?

work. She helped Michael add detail to his pictures and his stories so he would be able to articulate more about his stories and have an easier time recalling them. The interaction usually resulted in the teacher writing the well-developed story in a small, blank, teacher-made booklet (Duncan 2005). This booklet was the vehicle for the teacher to record the student's story using conventionally spelled words and to help her make her teaching points about how books and stories work.

After Michael completed the illustrations in his new book, he reread it to his teacher and his friends. Michael was excited to find that his teacher and his friends honored what he had to say by listening with care and interest. His interactions with Ms. Walker and fellow students began to change dramatically as the teaching and learning focused consistently on developing and extending his oral language through the stories he had to tell and the pictures he drew.

These school experiences prompted Janeen to reconsider her concerns about his attitude toward school. At one point early in Michael's kindergarten year, she beamed and commented, "Michael loves to learn. He sees a purpose to learning. The other day when Michael came home, he said, 'I got so much done today, Mom.' He is much more task oriented, and he is willing to follow through on his tasks." Despite the fact that Michael made great strides in his literacy development, Ms. Walker continued to be concerned about the gap between his performance and that of his peers. What was clear to Michael's kindergarten teacher and his mother was that if the prekindergarten experience had focused more on literacy development and learning, not just social or behavioral issues, a gap would have been less likely.

A BRIDGE BETWEEN PREKINDERGARTEN AND KINDERGARTEN

If prekindergarten or kindergarten teachers do not view their students as beginning readers and writers the minute they walk through the door, then students do not receive the kind of instruction that is developmentally appropriate for literacy learning. Unless the classroom is supportive of the student in relation to all areas of development, including literacy, the student will not be fully prepared for the school journey that lies ahead.

What should the first school experience look like if it is to serve as a literacy bridge? What would the literacy assessment and instruction have looked like for Michael if there had been a stronger connection between prekindergarten and kindergarten?

Marie Clay, a noted teacher and researcher from New Zealand, believes that the early years should lay the foundation for literacy learning and that there should be a strong connection between what happens in prekindergarten or kindergarten and the later years. She states:

> It is also easy to detect a chasm between the aims of preschools and schools. An early childhood position might be let them play and explore and enjoy their early childhood. A school's position might prepare children for literacy learning. We need a bridge over these troubled waters—troubled waters found across the world—between preschool and school literacy. . . .Preschool environments should provide opportunities for literacy events to occur, and adults should interact with literacy awareness shown by the child. In both preschool and school every adult should be

- What foundation do I need to provide for the children in my classroom for them to be successful as they progress through the grades?

- What connection should I make for these children between the prekindergarten and kindergarten experience and beyond?

alert to any response that a learner is making to literate things, to grab the moment and go with the interest, in some way interact with it, lead it on a little, and then let it go.

If preschools do not try to provide opportunities they will see little literacy awareness, and if they deliberately ignore it they provide children with models of people who ignore literate activities (Clay 1998, 199).

Chapter 2 looks at several prekindergarten/kindergarten perspectives and assesses their impact on literacy learning. It asks the question, "Are these perspectives focused enough on literacy to help support the goals in education today?" The chapter also looks at current research and begins to lay a framework in which to begin a look at developmentally appropriate assessment and instruction as it relates to early literacy development.

Chapter 2 How Theoretical Perspectives Influence Assessment and Instruction

Effective teaching depends upon the idea that teachers have an understanding of where their children have been, where they are, and where they are going as learners. While there are useful learning elements from most perspectives, there are more effective, engaging, and authentic ways for literacy instruction to happen in the prekindergarten/kindergarten classroom. Because what teachers believe about learning influences how and what they teach, we examine several broad prekindergarten/kindergarten perspectives. We ask if any of them are focused enough—or go far enough—to help support literacy learning. We believe that *all* students deserve assessment-driven instruction that focuses on their literacy development and is developmentally appropriate.

GUIDING QUESTIONS

- What is the focus of the teaching in my classroom?
- How and why have I chosen that particular focus?
- How does this focus impact the way I currently assess and teach children?

- What is the focus of the teaching in my classroom?

- How and why have I chosen that particular focus?

- How does this focus impact the way I currently assess and teach children?

CURRENT PERSPECTIVES ON PREKINDERGARTEN/KINDERGARTEN INSTRUCTION

There is a diverse range of theoretical perspectives that direct the focus of what's important to assess, teach, and learn in prekindergarten/kindergarten classrooms. This range of thinking has added to the ongoing discussions of what developmentally appropriate assessment and instruction means for the youngest learners as they enter a formalized educational setting. Most current prekindergarten/kindergarten classrooms can be categorized into one of three perspectives: play-centered classrooms, academic classrooms, and exploratory classrooms.

Although many classrooms may incorporate some aspect of each perspective, it is usually possible to determine a teacher's primary belief system based upon observing the classroom environment and the teacher/child interactions. The following descriptions briefly outline three perspectives: the **play perspective,** the **academic perspective,** and the **exploratory perspective.** The implication of identifying each perspective separately is not to say that they are mutually exclusive of one another, but to show that they focus on different aspects of learning. Regardless of the classroom perspective, students' can experience gaps similar to the one Michael experienced.

The Play Perspective
In **play-centered** classrooms, children are engaged in play activities in which the main emphasis is on social/emotional and physical development. A belief that supports this type of environment is that later academic success is primarily dependent on the child's social/emotional and physical development. Here the classroom is set

up to engage the student in a variety of play activities, with an emphasis on interacting socially. The teacher in this type of classroom spends time observing and recording the social/emotional and physical development of each child. A daily schedule might include the following:

> 8:45-9:05 TABLE-TOP ACTIVITIES
>
> Activities include puzzles, stringing beads, games, interlocking blocks, modeling clay, drawing materials, stamps and ink pads, water colors.
>
> 9:05-9:20 RUG TIME
>
> Activities include Current Events, Show and Tell, and Calendar.
>
> 9:20-10:05 CHOICE TIME
>
> Activities include sand and water table, the gym, creative play area, block area, library and puppet area, paint easels, and fine motor games.
>
> 10:05-10:20 CLEAN-UP—BATHROOM/HAND WASHING
>
> 10:20-10:35 SNACK
>
> 10:35-10:50 CLEAN-UP—BATHROOM/HAND WASHING
>
> 10:50-11:15 COOPERATIVE ACTIVITY
>
> Activities include parachute games, bean bag games, rhythm and movement games, songs and finger plays and games such as The Farmer in the Dell.
>
> 11:15-11:30 STORY AND GOOD-BYE SONG

The Academic Perspective

Due to increased state and federal guidelines for academic achievement in schools, **academic perspectives** have become more and more popular with both politicians and parents. Children in this type of environment are engaged in activities that develop the academic skills (primarily reading/phonics and math), which are assumed to

- What is the focus of the teaching in my classroom?

- How and why have I chosen that particular focus?

- How does this focus impact the way I currently assess and teach children?

be necessary for success in later educational settings. A belief of the teacher in this prekindergarten or kindergarten setting is that children are in need of teaching and capable of learning at an earlier age. These teachers believe that if children are to become successful in reading, writing, and math, there should be early and direct instruction. This type of direct instruction is usually supplied through a purchased program or a basal which takes all students through a lock-step progression of skills at the same time. This academic approach is not a "wait and see" philosophy.

The following description is an example of a program in an academic prekindergarten classroom:

> ... We offer a learning environment that incorporates a variety of the integral curriculum areas in order to maximize the learning potential of each child. Curriculum is activity centered, involving both teacher and children in the learning process. "Animal Island," an exceptional reading readiness program, introduces the letters and sounds of the alphabet; "Math Their Way" develops understanding of mathematical patterns and principles through the use of concrete materials and problem solving. During this important year of a child's development, we thoroughly prepare our four year olds for a successful transition into kindergarten.

The daily schedule of this academic classroom is similar to aspects of the play-centered classroom but includes a strong emphasis on the curriculum areas mentioned in the description. The daily schedule in an academic environment would incorporate a specific time for the explicit teaching of reading and/or phonics and math. These subjects would be taught to students daily or on a rotating, every other day, basis.

The Exploratory Perspective

Teachers in **exploratory type** classrooms plan different activities so that children may explore, experience, and interact with the materials provided. These activities are designed to further develop what are considered to be the natural interests of the child. Exploratory classrooms provide situations where teachers observe the child, record his or her strengths, and develop outcomes based on those observations. This perspective represents the idea that children grow from their natural interests and, as a result, other interests will develop. A description from one such preschool classroom reads:

> In our preschool and kindergarten programs, each classroom is a unique learning environment for a variety of reasons. Children move periodically to special rooms for science, the arts, language, and construction. This integrated approach helps to broaden each child's learning journey. Projects can be continued day to day if necessary, rather than beginning and ending on the same day. This approach allows children to investigate an idea in depth rather than being on a time-specific schedule. Learning takes place both on the inside and outside of school. A project may begin outside while the class is engaged in water play. The children may then move the learning indoors into the Science Lab to better investigate the topic, using microscopes, gauges, and scales. The Art Studio provides media from paint to paper to clay and recyclables for further exploration. The project may then be acted out in the Sound Stage room, or explored through the customs of other cultures in the World Markets room.

- What is the focus of the teaching in my classroom?

- How and why have I chosen that particular focus?

- How does this focus impact the way I currently assess and teach children?

Learning is a journey, both throughout the school and through the children's initiatives.

The structure of the exploratory classroom differs vastly from the play-centered or academic classroom. The focus in this classroom is on supporting children as they more fully develop their individual interests in any area within the classroom or, as in this description, throughout the school.

RETHINKING PREKINDERGARTEN/ KINDERGARTEN PERSPECTIVES

When considering these examples of different theoretical perspectives, it is apparent that they make a difference to the teaching and learning that occurs in the classroom. All three perspectives *attempt* to link their teaching to where children have come from and where they are developmentally, but effective teaching also depends upon the idea that teachers have a strong understanding of where students are going as learners. Are these three classrooms' perspectives focused enough to help support the goals in education today? For example, reading and writing are major focuses of schools and educational standards alike. A student's control of the basic skills in reading and writing are probably *the* single most important factor in how successful he or she will be within any school experience, and subsequently, throughout life. How do these three philosophies directly support a child's development in learning to read and write? In considering these ideas, then how do prekindergarten or kindergarten classrooms support the developing reader and writer in age-appropriate ways? Modern kindergarten classrooms are often the first formally structured educational setting in which many children will experience reading and writing instruction. For Michael, kindergarten was not his first school experience. Even though he attended prekindergarten, Michael did not seem to have the necessary experiences to fully support him as he entered kindergarten. With his experiences in mind, the question arises, "What should effective instruction look like if it is to support the developing reader and writer?"

Many well-known researchers and organizations around the world have given educators supportive guidelines to help focus beginning literacy instruction. Marie Clay suggests that, whether children learn these things at home or in preschool or in a combination, they will be appropriately prepared to enter school if they have:

- developed a good control of oral language
- taken an interest in the visual detail of their environment
- reached the level of experience which enables them to coordinate what they hear in language and what they see in print
- acquired enough movement flexibility, or motor coordination of hand and eye, to learn to control the directional movement patterns required for reading (1991, 41).

The International Reading Association/National Association of Educators of Young Children (IRA/NAEYC) joint position statement on preschool literacy points out that:

Young children need developmentally appropriate experiences and teaching to support literacy learning. These include but are not limited to:

- positive nurturing relationships with adults who engage in responsive conversations with individual children...

- What is the focus of the teaching in my classroom?

- How and why have I chosen that particular focus?

- How does this focus impact the way I currently assess and teach children?

- print-rich environments that provide opportunities and tools for children to see and use written language...
- adults' daily reading of high quality books to individual children or small groups...
- opportunities for children to talk about what is read...
- teaching strategies and experiences that develop phonemic awareness...
- opportunities to engage in play that incorporates literacy tools...
- first hand experiences that expand children's vocabulary... (Neuman, Copple, and Bredekamp 2000, 16).

In looking over these guidelines it is clear that some aspects of the three different perspectives previously discussed (play-centered, academic, and exploratory) are evident, but what is also clear is that these guidelines highlight the need for a language-rich and visually stimulating environment as the focal points of beginning literacy instruction.

Chapter 3 addresses the current research on beginning literacy instruction and applies it to the characteristics of emergent readers and writers—the foundation of literacy learning. Using the precursors of emergent readers and writers, oral language development and attention to visual detail, this chapter makes a case for developmentally appropriate literacy instruction based on our understandings of those areas, with a focus on assessment, teaching, and learning in prekindergarten or kindergarten.

Chapter 3

Exploring Characteristics of Emergent Readers and Writers

This chapter looks at strengthening the connection between the child's first school experience and later ones, and it explores ways to use oral language and visual detail as a vehicle for literacy assessment and instruction. While certain aspects of each of the three perspectives described in Chapter 2 have a place in any prekindergarten or kindergarten classroom, none of them go far enough to support the literacy development of children. It is through a deep understanding of the **Characteristics of Emergent Readers and Writers** and assessment-driven practice that teachers of young children can begin to support their learners.

GUIDING QUESTIONS

- What do I already know and understand about the development of readers and writers?
- What is a developmentally appropriate focus for readers and writers in my classroom?

CHARACTERISTICS OF EMERGENT LANGUAGE USERS

To begin an examination of early literacy instruction, teachers first need to look at child development in relation to oral language, reading, and writing. These three processes include broad developmental

- What do I already know and understand about the development of readers and writers?

- What is a developmentally appropriate focus for readers and writers in my classroom?

stages ranging from *emergent to early to fluent*. Within each stage of reading and writing development there are helpful characteristics that define the attitudes, understandings, and behaviors of children. Oral language underpins the development of readers and writers and is highly related to understanding and using the **Early Literacy Continuum.**

LINKING ORAL LANGUAGE AND VISUAL DETAIL TO EMERGENT READERS AND WRITERS

Most descriptors of emergent readers and writers deal primarily with oral language and the use of pictures. For very young children, reading and writing are mainly oral language activities. Pictures are the main source of information that emergent readers and writers use as they begin to read and write. With that in mind, oral language and attention to visual/picture detail are essential for success in beginning literacy development. **The better children's oral language and their attention to detail within pictures, the stronger the foundation they build for reading and writing.**

What was the foundation that was being built in Michael's prekindergarten experience? How would Michael's prekindergarten experience have been different if his teacher had based the instruction on these understandings? Given that Michael's kindergarten teacher had concerns with his oral language, a focus on oral language development and attention to visual/picture detail in prekindergarten might have made a significant impact on Michael's learning in kindergarten. With assessments in the areas of oral language development and attention to visual/picture detail, the teacher and Michael's parents might have worked more effectively together to better support Michael in his literacy development.

CHARACTERISTICS OF EMERGENT READERS

The following is a list of characteristics of emergent readers. These characteristics are adapted from *Developing Life-long Readers* (Mooney 1988) and are important for prekindergarten and kindergarten teachers to know and understand because they underpin the **Teaching Objectives** section of the **Early Literacy Continuum** (see Chapter 4).

This list of characteristics is divided into three sections: attitudes toward reading, understandings about reading, and behaviors as readers. Attitudes and understandings are an important part of the emergent reading and writing experience. The attitudes and understandings students hold can only be assessed through observing their behaviors. Thus the continuum deals with behaviors of the student. Attitudes have to do with how students feel about the act of reading. Understandings relate to what the reader knows about the act of reading. Behaviors show which attitudes and understandings the reader possesses.[1]

Attitudes toward Reading

- Is eager to hear and use new language
- Shows pleasure in the rhyme and rhythm of language
- Enjoys "playing" with language
- Is eager to listen to stories, rhymes, and poems
- Expects books to amuse, delight, comfort, and excite
- Has an attitude of anticipation and expectancy about books and stories
- Expects to make sense of what is read to him/her and what she/he reads
- Is eager to return to some books

[1]Margaret Mooney has also written about the characteristics of emergent readers and writers in *Books for Young Learners Teacher Resource* (2003) and *Literacy Learning: Teachers as Professional Decision Makers* (2004b).

- What do I already know and understand about the development of readers and writers?

- What is a developmentally appropriate focus for readers and writers in my classroom?

- Is eager to respond to some stories
- Wants to read and sees him- or herself as a reader
- Is confident in making an attempt
- Responds to feedback

Understandings about Reading

- Knows language can be recorded and revisited
- Knows how stories and books work
- Thinks about what may happen and uses this to unfold the story
- Understands that the texts, as well as the illustrations, carry the story
- Recognizes book language and sometimes uses this in speech, retellings, writing, or play
- Understands the importance of background knowledge and uses this to get meaning
- Knows the reward of reading and rereading
- Experiences success, which drives the child to further reading
- Is aware of some print conventions

Behaviors as Readers

- Plays at reading
- Handles books confidently
- Interprets pictures
- Uses pictures to predict text
- Retells a known story in sequence
- Develops a memory for text
- Finger-points to locate specific words
- Focuses on some detail
- Identifies some words
- Hears sound sequence in words
- Uses some letter-sound links

- Rereads to regain meaning
- Explores new books
- Returns to favorite books
- Chooses to read independently at times.

CHARACTERISTICS OF EMERGENT WRITERS

The following list is adapted from *Dancing with the Pen: The Learner as a Writer* (New Zealand Ministry of Education 1992) and describes some of the characteristics of emergent writers. These characteristics also link strongly to the **Teaching Objectives** portion of the continuum. As with reading, the list of writing characteristics is divided into three sections: attitudes toward writing, understandings about writing, and behaviors as writers. Note the similarities between the characteristics of readers and the characteristics of writers, and how they relate to the development of oral language. For example, in the **Behavior as Readers** section, one of the characteristics is "Interprets pictures" while in the **Behaviors as Writers** section, one finds "Explains orally about own pictures." Because oral language plays such an integral part in the development of the emergent reader and writer, there is a close connection between the characteristics of these two areas.

Attitudes toward Writing
- Is eager to play at writing
- Has confidence that personal experience is expressed with meaning in own writing
- Is encouraged by own success to write again
- Expects writing to be enjoyable
- Finds writing rewarding
- Expects own writing to belong to self

- What do I already know and understand about the development of readers and writers?

- What is a developmentally appropriate focus for readers and writers in my classroom?

Understandings about Writing
- Print holds meaning
- Stories can be written down
- Speech can be written down
- Writing can be read over and over again
- Begins to understand that thoughts can be written down
- Is responsible for own topics and learning
- Is developing an understanding of how books and stories work
- Is learning to write by watching the teacher's models and from own knowledge of familiar texts
- Expects the teacher to help in developing text
- Begins to realize that words are always spelled the same

Behaviors as Writers
- Orients a page to start writing
- Develops some knowledge of directionality, spaces between words, upper and lower case letters
- Uses own experiences for writing
- Is beginning to locate references, such as students' names
- Centers topics largely on own world
- Draws pictures and scribbles to generate and express ideas
- Explains orally about own pictures
- Is able to make corrections when text is read back by the teacher
- Asks questions about others' stories
- Adds on to own story
- Experiments with letter shapes to arrive at consistency of letter form
- Uses pictures as a basis for writing

- Is prepared to attempt the spelling of unknown words by taking risks
- Shows some knowledge of alphabet through production of letter forms to represent message; develops sound-letter relationships
- Can recognize a few key words
- Has control of some essential words.

CONSIDERING A RANGE OF CAPABILITY

It would not be appropriate to expect all students to exhibit all of these characteristics. While some prekindergarten or kindergarten students might not yet exhibit all of the characteristics listed, others may be ready to go beyond them. For those students, we recommend that teachers further consult books and resources such as *Developing Life-long Readers* (Mooney 1988), *Dancing with the Pen: The Learner as a Writer* (New Zealand Ministry of Education 1992), *Reading for Life: The Learner as a Reader* (New Zealand Ministry of Education 1997), and *Books for Young Learners Teacher Resource* (Mooney 2003). It is important to keep in mind the characteristics of the other broad, overlapping stages of early and fluent reading and writing development found in these resources because effective teaching depends upon understanding where children have been, where they are currently, and where they need to go as learners.

Focused early literacy instruction is essential in building a solid foundation for future literacy development. If attention to picture detail and oral language is the solid foundation, then how is a student's ability to notice detail in the environment developed? How is a student's oral language developed? The next 3 chapters demonstrate how the characteristics shown here support the **Early**

- What do I already know and understand about the development of readers and writers?

- What is a developmentally appropriate focus for readers and writers in my classroom?

Literacy Continuum. The information in these chapters allows teachers to plan for intentional and effective literacy instruction in ways that young children can enjoy and value.

The **Early Literacy Continuum** is used for both assessing and teaching. Chapter 4 describes the different areas of the continuum and, in particular, looks at how the continuum can and should be used when assessing a student's oral language and the detail in his or her work. Recommendations for both administering and scoring of the results of the assessments are also given.

SECTION II   UNDERSTANDING HOW TO USE THE EARLY LITERACY CONTINUUM

Chapter 4

Using the Early Literacy Continuum

This chapter introduces a continuum that supports the development of the emergent reader and writer in developmentally appropriate ways. This continuum, when used properly, helps match up assessment with classroom practice. Because of this alignment between assessment and classroom practice, teaching becomes more focused.

GUIDING QUESTION

- How can I monitor and assess my students' oral language development and attention to detail?

Oral language and attention to picture detail are critical for literacy development in young children. Assessment of these precursors to reading and writing is fundamental to literacy development. Teachers need to understand where their students are in relation to oral language development and attention to picture detail, and teachers need to know how to monitor for growth in these areas. The **Early Literacy Continuum** is a tool that can help teachers do that. This tool helps teachers use observation of daily classroom activities in a systematic and ongoing way.

UNDERSTANDING THE EARLY LITERACY CONTINUUM

The **Early Literacy Continuum**, displayed in Figure 4.1, consists of three distinct sections. The two outer sections of the continuum focus on oral language development and student work.

Early Literacy Continuum

Level of Student's Work	Teaching Objectives	Level of Student's Oral Language[1] (in the language of instruction)
1. The student's work consists of scribbles, random shapes, or exploration of materials. It is not recognizable.	**Through conversation and by the student adding on to his/her work, the student will be able to:** • See Figure 4.2 for details. • • • • •	1. The student will not converse about his or her work. However, he or she may gesture.
2. The student's work is only recognizable when the student talks about it.		2. The student gives one word, a short phrase, or a simple sentence about his or her work through teacher questioning. However, the student may seem unsure and/or give different responses during continued conversation.
3. The student's work is recognizable, but lacks important detail that is critical to the story.	**The student will add on to his/her own work and will be able to:** • See Figure 4.3 for details. • (Teacher will take dictation.)	3. The student gives one word, short phrases, or a simple sentence about his or her work. The language remains constant during the conversation and over time.
4. The student's work contains important detail that is critical to the story, but lacks "writing."		4. The student is able to tell a story about his or her work through teacher questioning.
5. The student's work contains important detail that is critical to the story and includes "writing."	**In the student's journal or writing book, the student will be able to:** • See Figure 4.4 for details. • • •	5. The student is able to tell a simple story about his or her work with little or no teacher support.

© 2005 by Deborah K. Freeman and David M. Matteson

[1]In ELL/ESL and bilingual classrooms, dictation is taken in the language of instruction. For example, in a Spanish bilingual classroom, the language of instruction is Spanish. In any ELL/ESL classroom, the language of instruction is English.

Figure 4.1: Early Literacy Continuum

The Student's Oral Language section deals with a student's ability to tell a story as it relates to his or her own work. This section consists of five boxes that represent five different developmental levels of a student's current ability to tell a story.

The Student Work section focuses on the student's attention to detail in his or her work. This section consists of five boxes that represent five developmental levels of a student's current ability to add detail to his or her work.

The third section, Teaching Objectives, consists of three separate boxes in the middle of the continuum where any state or district goals can be placed in order to plan for teaching that responds to each child's developmental level in the Student Oral Language section and Student Work section of the continuum. Also, using the Characteristics of Emergent Readers and Writers (Chapter 3) as a guide can enhance the Teaching Objectives section. Depending upon the thoroughness and appropriateness of individual state or district goals, the behavior portion of the emergent characteristics of readers and writers could be utilized as objectives. There is a *strong* connection between the Student's Oral Language, Student's Work, and Teaching Objectives sections of the continuum. The lines that connect the boxes within the continuum represent these connections.

USING THE THREE TEACHING OBJECTIVE BOXES

In the Teaching Objectives section, the uppermost box represents teaching to develop a child's oral language and improve the student work through conversation between the teacher and the student. The example in Figure 4.2, excerpted from Figure 4.1, shows where objectives that are taught through conversation should be placed.

• How can I monitor and assess my students' oral language development and attention to detail?

> **Through conversation and by the student adding on to his/her work, the student will be able to:**
> • stay on topic
> • identify character(s) and/or event(s) of a story
> • retell some sequence of events
> • make connections to self, others, and/or environment
> • use both real and make-believe situations
> • answer questions
> • ask questions and make comments on work
> • apply knowledge/experiences to new areas (drawing, painting, blocks, housekeeping, etc.).

Figure 4.2: Objectives Taught Through Conversation

The second box in this section, shown in Figure 4.3, represents teaching through the taking of dictation. Through this approach of taking dictation, the teacher records all or part of the student's story that most clearly connects to the picture. The teacher chooses to take dictation based upon one of the objectives listed in either of the first two boxes of the Teaching Objectives section of the continuum.

> **The student will add on to his/her own work and will be able to:**
> • tell a simple story, focusing on favorite or most important part. (Teacher will take dictation.)

Figure 4.3: Taking Dictation Based on Objectives

The last box in the Teaching Objectives section represents teaching through students' writing. The state or district's goals are organized according to where they would most likely fit within this developmental flow. The arrows that connect the boxes in this section represent this flow (see Figure 4.4).

In the student's journal or writing book, the student will be able to:
- understand that the illustration holds most of the meaning when reading text
- use letter/letter-like symbols to represent writing
- understand that writing has a purpose
- recognize the connection between the spoken and written word
- identify letters
- connect sounds to their letters
- understand some concepts about print

Figure 4.4: Teaching Writing Based on Objectives

Arrows connect the three boxes of this section. These arrows represent the flexibility of utilizing objectives among the approaches of conversation, dictation, or student's journal writing. The approach would change depending on the student's developmental level. However, a teacher who is taking dictation from a student may use one of the objectives from the second box but may also have the option to use objectives from the first box if appropriate to the teaching.

- How can I monitor and assess my students' oral language development and attention to detail?

GENERAL DIRECTIONS FOR ASSESSING

The Early Literacy Continuum is used for both assessment and teaching. Because we believe that assessment precedes teaching, a discussion of the continuum as an assessment tool comes before the discussion of its implications for teaching. We recommend collecting assessment data every four to six weeks, but certainly no less than three to four times a year. The more current the assessment, the more focused and intentional the instruction can be.

When teachers use the continuum for assessing, they should ensure that students do not borrow or share ideas from one another. In order to get a more accurate snapshot of what the student knows, the teacher wants to be sure that it is the child's own work and story that are being assessed and evaluated. When we assess, we work right in the classroom. The assessment we have developed very closely resembles the everyday work in which our students are involved. During an assessment the student is given a blank piece of drawing paper and crayons then asked to draw a picture. The amount of time needed for the child to complete the drawing will depend on the developmental level of the student. For example, a child who is on level one and is scribbling may only spend a minute or two on the drawing. A child who is on level four and uses more detail might spend five or more minutes on the drawing. Once the student has completed the picture, the teacher says, "Tell me about your picture." It usually takes no more than three to five minutes to hear about the picture or for the student to tell the story. The teacher makes some observation notes by jotting down a brief written description of the picture as well as a short note about the oral interaction. These notes will help later when evaluating the assessment sample. The more complete the notes, the faster the evaluation will go.

After the student has talked about his or her picture or the story, the teacher asks, "Is your picture finished?" A caution is to remain a neutral observer and not interfere with the student's work at this time. The Assessment Guide in Figure 4.5 was designed to help bring consistency to the assessment procedure when using the **Early Literacy Continuum.**

The Early Literacy Continuum Assessment Guide

1. Ask students to make a picture with materials that they are already familiar with using. For example: If the student has not used watercolors in the past, do *not* give him/her watercolors for the first time when you ask him/her to draw this picture.

2. Do *not* prompt the student about the work that is being completed. Questions are likely to be interpreted as instructional prompts. For example, do *not* ask: "Where is your mommy in the picture?" or "What about your hair?"

3. When the student has completed the drawing ask, "Tell me about your picture."

4. Write down the student's response to your request.

5. Read the student's response back and ask: "Is there anything else that you want to add to your picture?"

6. If the student responds yes, allow the student to include more details and add the student's additional words to what you previously wrote. Sometimes after hearing their own words read back to them, students will decide that they wish to add more details to the picture and/or the explanation. *Never* push the student to do so, simply ask the question as given in #5.

7. The actual Early Literacy Continuum Individual Student Recording Sheet that you complete will be placed in each student's file with the student work sample the assessment is based upon.

8. The student's scores will be recorded on The Early Literacy Continuum Classroom Summary Sheet. It is this sheet that will be turned in to the district.

Adapted from Cartwright Preschool

Figure 4.5: Directions for Administering the Early Literacy Assessment

- How can I monitor and assess my students' oral language development and attention to detail?

GENERAL DIRECTIONS FOR EVALUATING STUDENT WORK

When using the **Early Literacy Continuum** to evaluate a piece of student work, teachers should be conservative in how they rate the student's work or oral language on the continuum. When it is difficult to decide which level to assign the student's work or the student's oral language, it is prudent to rate the student at the lower level since expectations at the higher level may later cause frustration for the teacher and the child during the daily teaching. A student's best learning likely occurs when the teacher is in the student's Zone of Proximal Development (ZPD), which is defined as "the distance between the actual developmental level as determined by individual problem-solving and the level of potential development as determined through problem-solving under adult guidance or in collaboration with more capable peers" (Vygotsky 1978, 86). In other words, the ZPD is what children can *almost* do by themselves but still need some instructional assistance from the teacher or other peers in order to be successful. For that reason, it is crucial that teachers use caution when rating a student's work. The teacher's aim should always be to stay within the student's ZPD. The scoring considerations in Figure 4.6 offer some guidelines to use when assessing students.

This chapter looked at using the **Early Literacy Continuum** to administer a formal assessment several times during the school year. The goal at these times is only to gather information; teaching occurs later. These assessments help determine a student's skill level at a point in time, and to show student growth over time.

The Early Literacy Continuum Scoring Considerations

Student's Work:

1. Be objective when scoring the work sample. The score given *will not* be used to determine the effectiveness or the abilities of the teacher. The score is used *only* to measure children's progress over time.

2. Sometimes you may find that you have difficulty choosing between one score and the next higher number. When this occurs, *always* choose the lower number.

3. Even when the student draws shapes that are recognizable, if you are unable to figure out the purpose for the objects without an explanation, then the score is a 1.

4. Sometimes it really helps to confer with a colleague, especially one who has knowledge of the student. Often through discussion you will be able to form conclusions that you might not come to on your own.

Oral Language:

1. The assessment is designed to measure oral language development in English. If the student describes his or her drawing in Spanish, those words are recorded in Spanish. The student is then asked to describe his or her drawing in English. Those words are recorded as well. The teacher will plan for individualized instruction based upon the student's response or responses.

2. It is best practice to write an observation recording the student's words that were given in Spanish because although you won't use the Spanish words in this assessment, you certainly will use the student's details in your planning for individualization.

3. As in the case of the work sample, when in doubt between two scores, always choose the lower score.

4. As in the case of the work sample, do not prompt the student or press for more details. Simply offer the opportunity to add details. If the student declines, end the activity and score based upon what has been provided.

Adapted from Cartwright Preschool

Figure 4.6: Directions for Scoring the Early Literacy Assessment

• How can I monitor and assess my students' oral language development and attention to detail?

Another aspect of using this continuum is to aid a teacher in selecting appropriate teaching objectives. Assessment for the purpose of selecting teaching objectives involves a more in-depth evaluation. This in-depth evaluation is made after the teacher has already obtained an **Oral Language** level and a **Student Work** level. It is at this point that we need to choose one of the objectives contained within the **Teaching Objectives** section of the continuum. When the teacher has an idea of a student's developmental levels, the teacher can begin to select objectives that support a child's needs based on the child's work. The chosen objective will guide and focus the conversation between the teacher and the student. To illustrate the look and sound of student work and oral language that is ranked at the different levels of the continuum, see the vignettes in Chapters 5 and 6. For more on teaching objectives, see Chapter 7.

Chapter 5

Implications for Developing Students' Work

Because noticing and using detail is an important aspect in a child's literacy development, this chapter takes an in-depth look at teachers working with students in order to develop detail within student work. Even though there is a close connection between a student's work and a student's oral language, for clarity we focus only on student work in this chapter. Chapter 6 focuses on oral language as it relates to student work.

The following vignettes show teachers interacting with students and their work. They include samples of student work accomplished during those teaching episodes. The purpose of the vignettes is to help teachers clarify each level of the continuum and to show how they can support their students' learning along a continuum. This chapter focuses on teachers helping students develop their work. It is the student work that will serve as a springboard for the conversation that the teacher uses to develop the student's oral language. These vignettes can also help teachers understand how to evaluate student work as they take assessments, either formally (refer to the instructions in Chapter 4 for formal assessment procedures) or informally as they teach and reassess on the spot.

GUIDING QUESTIONS

- Where are my students on the broad developmental levels of the continuum in relation to including detail within their work?

- Where are my students on the broad developmental levels of the continuum in relation to including detail within their work?

- Do my interactions with students have clear and focused objectives that ultimately move my students through a learning continuum?

- Do my interactions with students have clear and focused objectives that ultimately move my students through a learning continuum?

EXPLORING LEVELS OF PROFICIENCY IN STUDENT WORK

Student work does not refer just to pictures. With most students there is a close connection between the pictures they draw and the constructions they make. For example, those students who lack detail in their pictures often lack the same kind of detail in their constructions. The similarities found in pictures can also be found in constructions in the block area, at the clay table, and at the painting easel. Teachers can preserve valuable information by taking photographs of constructions. Anything a student creates can be evaluated and developed. The following vignettes, drawn from several real classrooms, have examples of attention to detail in both pictures and constructions.

STUDENT WORK AT LEVEL 1

The student's work consists of scribbles, random shapes, or exploration of materials. It is not recognizable.

1. The student's work consists of scribbles, random shapes, or exploration of materials. It is not recognizable.

The student work that is ranked as Level 1 is often the easiest to identify but possibly the most challenging with which to work. Children at this level usually spend little time in the act of drawing or constructing within a classroom center and they do not appear to spend much time thinking about what their work will represent. In the following example, notice how the teacher supports the student to determine her topic and help her make her picture more recognizable.

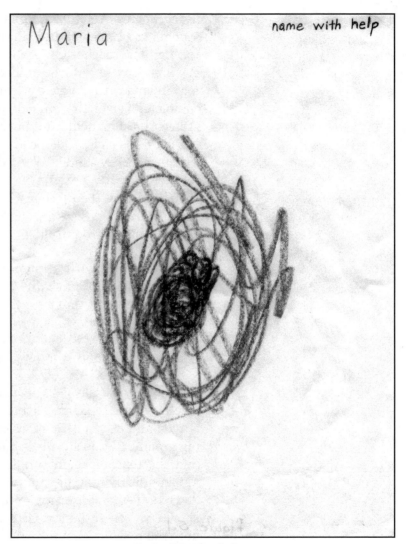

Figure 5.1: Maria's Drawing

- Where are my students on the broad developmental levels of the continuum in relation to including detail within their work?

- Do my interactions with students have clear and focused objectives that ultimately move my students through a learning continuum?

Maria comes over to the table where the teacher is waiting for three students to come and draw in their picture journals. She sits beside the teacher. The teacher gives Maria her journal and a container of markers and crayons. Maria immediately begins to make wide sweeping movements with a purple crayon. Her movements seem random as she completes her picture quickly (see Figure 5.1). Maria enthusiastically states, "I'm finished!" and begins to leave the table. The teacher calls her back and says, "Tell me about your picture." "I drawed," says Maria. The teacher responds, "What did you draw?" She says, "Purple." The teacher asks, "What did you draw that was purple?" Maria looks thoughtfully at the teacher. The teacher continues, "Well you know I've seen balloons that are purple. Barney is purple, and Kelly's (a friend of Maria's) pants are purple. But what was your purple picture about?"

When working with students at Level 1, the teacher understands that they may not have any particular ideas behind the scribble. The teacher may find that he needs to give the student suggestions that will fit within the picture and the child's prior knowledge. Many times the child will choose one of the suggestions. The teacher, as necessary, will help add one important detail to the child's scribble.

Smiling, Maria says, "It's Barney!" The teacher playfully questions, "Well, where is Barney's big green belly?" Maria grabs the green crayon and uses a little more care when it comes to drawing Barney's big green belly, as shown in the color plate of Figure 5.1. Both Maria and the teacher seem satisfied with the results of the interaction. Maria quickly marches to the classroom library and the teacher jots down a few monitoring notes about his interaction with Maria, shown in Figure 5.2. Monitoring notes capture the interaction and help the teacher plan for what Maria will benefit from learning next.

Name: *Maria*   Date: *9/15*

Activity/Center: *Picture Journal*

Current Student Work Level: /

Current Oral Language Level: /

Notes
Student: *Impulsive-drew purple scribbles; did not talk about drawing*

Teacher: *Suggested topics for drawings-balloons, Barney, Kelly's pants; Prompted to add green belly after Maria chose Barney topic*

Next Step: *Need to start developing topic before activity-Talk with Maria about possible ideas to develop more detailed picture and show her how to add detail*

Figure 5.2: Monitoring Notes on a Level 1 Student

- Where are my students on the broad developmental levels of the continuum in relation to including detail within their work?

- Do my interactions with students have clear and focused objectives that ultimately move my students through a learning continuum?

---

2. The student's work is only recognizable when the student talks about it.

Should Maria not have chosen any of the teacher's suggestions, the teacher could have responded, "You think about what you drew that was purple, and I'll come back to talk with you in just a minute." But at this point the teacher has a crucial and on-the-spot decision to make. The teacher needs to reflect upon his last few interactions with Maria to decide what he will do if she does not come up with an idea for her picture. In this case, the teacher decides that he will encourage Maria to choose one of the suggested ideas for her purple scribble. He decides this because his goal is to help Maria *develop* a picture that represents something about her thoughts, feelings, or experiences. He also understands that focused teaching leads to focused learning.

STUDENT WORK AT LEVEL 2

The student's work is only recognizable when the student talks about it.

As in Level 1, the goal in Level 2 is to develop a picture or construction that represents something about the child's thoughts, feelings, or experiences. Unlike the scribbles of Level 1 the work at this level has more structure to it. Although the work is not easily recognizable to the teacher at first, parts can be identified when the student talks about it. As you read through the vignette, observe how the teacher encourages and supports the student to make the detail in the drawing even more noticeable.

Quentin sits at the writing center during free choice time. His teacher notices that he is spending a good deal of time working on his drawing. As the teacher approaches the table, Quentin says, "Do you want to see my picture?" She sits next to him and prepares to listen and take monitoring notes in order to record what happens as he talks about his drawing.

Through the course of the first few months of school, the teacher has set the tone in her classroom for this kind of interaction to occur naturally. It was her goal from the beginning of the year that students come to expect the teacher to converse with them about their work. Because she has consistently taken monitoring notes on student's work, she has clear objectives (see Figure 5.3) in mind and knows in advance what she needs to do to scaffold new learning for her students. The teacher is aware of the objectives that coincide with the continuum levels of student work, and she is prepared to work explicitly with her students regardless of their location or task within the classroom. The objectives, contained within this first box of the

The student will add detail to his or her work through:
- engaging in conversation (staying on topic and taking turns).
- identifying character(s) and/or event(s) of a story.
- beginning to retell some sequence of events in stories.
- asking questions and making comments about own work.
- telling a simple narrative, focusing on favorite or most memorable part.
- engaging in various forms of nonverbal communication with those who do not speak his or her home language (ESL).
- using single words and simple phrases to communicate meaning (ESL).
- attempting to use new vocabulary and grammar in speech (ESL).

Figure 5.3: Teaching Objectives for a Level 2 Student (See Arlington Adaptation on page 81.)

- Where are my students on the broad developmental levels of the continuum in relation to including detail within their work?

- Do my interactions with students have clear and focused objectives that ultimately move my students through a learning continuum?

Teaching Objectives section of the continuum, will guide the decision-making as the teacher works with her students.

The teacher asks, "What did you draw?" Quentin says, "It's my house." The house is drawn completely in yellow marker, making it difficult to see. Quentin's "structure" is lopsided with random scribbling inside. The roof is rounded and somewhat detached from the structure. The teacher wonders aloud, "What was happening at your house?" Quentin thinks for a moment and responds, "Daddy was gone. We couldn't get in the door." The teacher looks puzzled and asks, "Well, where's the door?" Quentin picks up the yellow marker and begins to add the door. The teacher says, "Do you think the door will show if you use yellow?" He nods his head yes. The teacher replies, "Okay, let's see." Quentin looks at the picture and makes a few more yellow marks on the yellow house. The teacher now suggests using another color so that the door will show. Quentin chooses a brown crayon, and the teacher takes his hand to help him draw the outline of the door (see Color Plate Figure 5.4).

The teacher understands that if a student's work is only recognizable when discussed "in the moment," it needs to have the specific detail added or developed that will *eventually* aid the student in remembering the story over time. Because the teacher understands the objectives that support student work at Level 2, she chooses the specific detail that she thinks will anchor the story in the child's mind. She chose the objective of "telling a simple narrative, focusing on favorite or most memorable part" (see Figure 5.3). As in the example, with Quentin the teacher encouraged the use of a different color to enhance the detail of the door. It is this detail of the door that will help the child recall and retell the story of being locked out of the house. The teacher realizes that the ultimate goal is for the student to add the

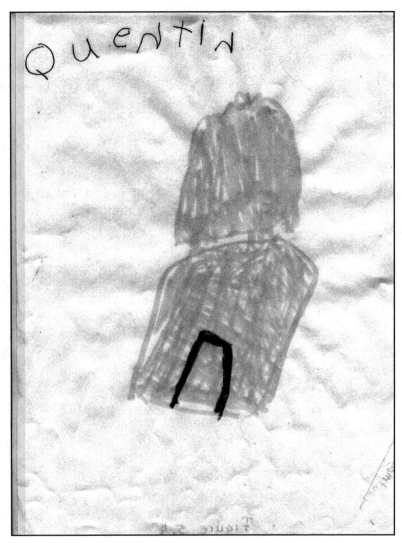

Figure 5.4: Quentin's Drawing of a House

important detail independently, and that she should offer support only when necessary. She also knows that at this point she needs to support the child further by taking his hand and helping him draw the door. Both of these efforts go a long way in helping Quentin develop and—the teacher hopes—remember what the important details in his picture mean and ultimately his story about it.

STUDENT WORK AT LEVEL 3

The student's work is recognizable, but lacks important detail that is critical to the story.

> 3. The student's work is recognizable, but lacks important detail that is critical to the story.

At Level 3, student work is characterized by a lack of the critical detail needed to remember the story over time. Young students often draw a picture that looks similar or identical to the pictures they have drawn previously. For example, many students draw pictures of family members, which frequently include people smiling and looking as if they are standing in mid-air with little to distinguish this picture from the last. One day the story may be that the family went swimming, on another day that the family went to the park and played on the swings, and on another the story may be the family went to the skating rink. The problem is that while the drawings of the people themselves may be very detailed, there is no critical detail—such as the setting of the swimming pool or the swing set—to distinguish one picture from another. It is this kind of critical detail that would aid the student in remembering the story over time. In the example below, notice how the teacher uses previous teaching interactions to support the current teaching.

Figure 5.1: Maria's Drawing

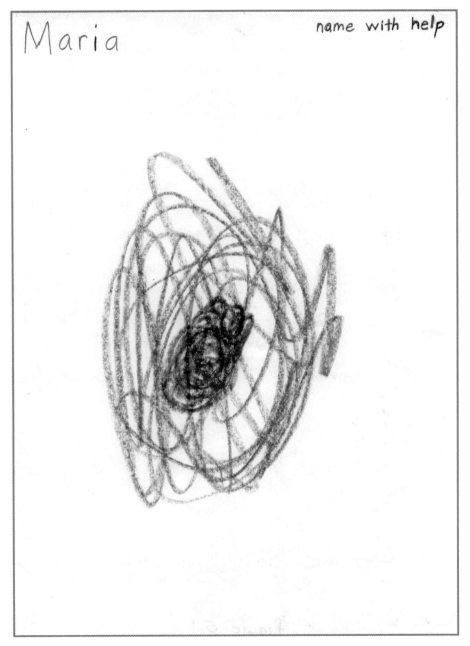

Figure 5.4: Quentin's Drawing of a House

Figure 5.5: Siena's Drawing of an Alligator Eating a Fish

SIENA

The alligator is eating the fish.

Figure 5.6: Siena's Drawing of an Alligator in the Sun

SIENA

The alligator is sitting in the sun.

Figure 5.7: Kenneth's Label on
His Zoo Construction

Figure 5.8: Keasha's Label on a
Bag of Cookies

Siena, four years of age, draws alligators every day for weeks. His detailed alligator drawings are outstanding, but he doesn't yet add the critical detail that will help him remember what the different alligator stories are about. On this day his response to the teacher's question, "Siena, what's happening here in your picture?" is "The alligator is sitting in the sun." However, he has not included the sun. The teacher thinks about his last story, "The alligator is eating the fish," (see Color Plate Figure 5.5) which initially had also lacked the critical detail of the fish.

The teacher understands that even though her student's pictures are very detailed and recognizable, they need to include details that differentiate one story from the other. It is the specific detail of the story that helps the student (and the teacher) recall and retell the story over time. This is especially important when the student's work is consistently based on a similar topic. In Siena's current story, it is the critical detail of the sun that will help him remember the story of an alligator in the sun.

The teacher now turns back to the last story, as shown in Figure 5.5, and asks Siena, "Do you remember this story?" He replies, "Yeah, that's about when the alligator eats the fish." The teacher smiles and asks, "How do you know that?" Siena says, " 'Cause I see the alligator eating the fish." His teacher replies, "That's right. Remember that you added the detail of the fish so we could remember the story. Now look at your drawing today. How will we remember that it's about the alligator sitting in the sun?" Siena grins, "Uh-Oh! I forgot the sun." He quickly flips back to today's story, grabs an orange crayon and adds a bright orange sun to his picture. (See Color Plate Figure 5.6)

- Where are my students on the broad developmental levels of the continuum in relation to including detail within their work?

- Do my interactions with students have clear and focused objectives that ultimately move my students through a learning continuum?

Figure 5.5: Siena's Drawing of an Alligator Eating a Fish

Figure 5.6: Siena's Drawing of an Alligator in the Sun

- Where are my students on the broad developmental levels of the continuum in relation to including detail within their work?

- Do my interactions with students have clear and focused objectives that ultimately move my students through a learning continuum?

The **Early Literacy Continuum** differs from traditional prekindergarten assessments such as a self-portrait in that the teacher also evaluates the details that are critical to the student's story. The teacher knows her students need to progress in how to represent a person in their drawings, but she also knows they need to develop their skill at noticing and adding critical detail to their story. Siena was successful in understanding which critical detail was missing because his teacher had been teaching him this concept at this level of the continuum over the last several weeks. The teacher understands that her students may remain at a particular level of the continuum for a period of time and may need repeated experiences for a particular learning objective. She also understands there is no expectation that all children will move through all the levels of the continuum or be on a particular level at a particular time. The expectation is that all children can and will make learning progress no matter where they start on the **Early Literacy Continuum.** This teacher also knows students will make the most progress when her teaching falls within each student's Zone of Proximal Development. The **Early Literacy Continuum** allows the teacher to individualize instruction for each student.

STUDENT WORK AT LEVEL 4

The student's work contains important detail that is critical to the story, but lacks "writing."

> 4. The student's work contains important detail that is critical to the story, but lacks "writing."

The student's work at level four contains both details in the individual objects and the detail necessary to support a more complex story. While this level continues to focus on incorporation of critical detail in the drawing or construction, the emphasis is on teaching the student to incorporate "writing" into his product. The teacher facilitates the student's understanding that print as well as the picture or construction will help carry the meaning. The student's text may be as simple as a single word or as long as one or two lines of print. The subtle shift at level four is from picture to print. Notice as you read how the teacher continues to support the student's movement through the Student's Work portion of the continuum even though the student has limited control of English.

Kenneth, a Vietnamese ESL student, spends almost all of his free choice time in the block center. Before it is time to clean up, the teacher approaches him to talk about his construction. Armed with knowledge from previous monitoring notes that provided a learning objective for Kenneth—"Needs to add writing to his work"—the teacher says, "Tell me about what you have built here." Kenneth quietly replies, "It zoo." Pointing to the interlocking blocks that had been tiered up the side of the block enclosure, the teacher asks, "What is this part here?" Kenneth responds, "Walk up," meaning they are stairs. The construction includes an arched entry leading into many compartments where zoo animal families have been placed. The detail is obvious given that each animal family has their own compartment. Around one side of the zoo Kenneth has lined up people. When his teacher asks, "What are these people doing?" He responds, "Look animals." At this point the teacher says, "The people are looking at the animals? Let's make a sign for your zoo." She offers Kenneth a piece of paper and a pencil that is kept in the block center for just such a purpose. He writes letters and tapes the sign over the arch.

His teacher is skillful enough to understand that Kenneth's work contains many more details than he can articulate in English at this

- Where are my students on the broad developmental levels of the continuum in relation to including detail within their work?

- Do my interactions with students have clear and focused objectives that ultimately move my students through a learning continuum?

Figure 5.7: Kenneth's Label on His Zoo Construction

time. She also knows that the continuum objectives can be met in any area of the classroom. Students need to be able to access writing material in all areas of the classroom, so the teacher sets up situations for writing to occur everywhere. By accepting what the student understands about writing such as the use of scribbles, letter-like forms, random letters, beginning or middle or ending sounds, or words, the student is more willing to take a risk and continue to write without being prompted by the teacher. All of the approximations that learners make—and that teachers use for instruction—bring them closer to becoming literate. All of the teacher interactions with Kenneth indicate her understanding that having a clear objective is essential if focused teaching is to occur.

STUDENT WORK AT LEVEL 5

The student's work contains important detail that is critical to the story, and includes "writing."

When students first reach this level they may or may not be including writing with their work. The focus at Level 5 is to have the students

> 5. The student's work contains important detail that is critical to the story, and includes "writing."

include writing on their work, regardless of the area of the classroom where the product was completed, such as pictures, blocks, clay, dramatic play, science, or art. This flexibility of writing in different areas and for different purposes increases the students' understanding that writing is meaningful. In the following vignette notice how the teacher encourages purposeful writing regardless of the topic of the student's work.

After many teaching episodes where the objective was to get Keasha to add writing to her pictures, she now consistently includes a string of random letters independently. At level five, the objective for Keasha is to be more flexible in her use of writing. Using writing in different areas will help Keasha understand that writing is a part of everyday experiences and has real purpose. Because several children in the class also need to develop this flexibility, the teacher chooses to use the clay center as a place for focused teaching. As he approaches the table, he notices that Keasha has created numerous disks of red clay that have caused a great deal of conversation. He hears her say, "I know they are Girl Scout cookies because my sister is selling some." Joining in the conversation, the teacher asks, "Who are the cookies for? Are they for us?" She confidently replies, "Noooo. I'm gonna sell them just like my sister." "Well if you want to sell them, you'll want to put them in a box and make a note to tell readers what kind of cookies they are." The teacher supplies a plastic bag, a self-sticking note pad, and a pencil. Then he says, "Since we don't have a box, you can use this plastic bag, and don't forget to write what kind of cookies they are."

Because the teacher knows that students need to be flexible in writing for various purposes, he understands that there are times when

- Where are my students on the broad developmental levels of the continuum in relation to including detail within their work?

- Do my interactions with students have clear and focused objectives that ultimately move my students through a learning continuum?

Figure 5.8: Keasha's Label on a Bag of Cookies

he must set up situations that encourage them to write in different areas of the classroom. Those areas need to be places where students are allowed to talk so that interactions will generate ideas from which writing will occur. He also knows that he needs to be observing student interactions to determine how and when to join in to meet his objective for any particular student. Even though the teacher sets up situations for learning to occur, he knows that he must follow the lead of the child if the activity is to remain meaningful.

These vignettes illustrate the idea that all of the teacher's interactions aim to move students along a learning continuum. Even though the learning may not be noticeably evident at the point of teaching, over time and with focused instruction, students will progress through the Student's Work levels of the continuum. The next chapter includes vignettes that will take a similar in-depth look at teacher/student interaction as students progress through the Oral Language levels of the continuum.

Chapter 6

Implications for Developing Students' Oral Language

As emphasized throughout this book, oral language is an important aspect in a child's literacy development. Because there is a close connection between a student's oral language and a student's other work, we found we could not effectively evaluate a student's work unless we also had the student tell us about his or her picture or construction. This chapter focuses on a student's oral language by looking at teachers working with students in order to develop the ability to tell a story. As in the previous chapter, the following vignettes show teachers interacting with students, but now we focus on the development of the student's oral language. Included in these vignettes are examples of anecdotal or monitoring notes of what occurred during these teaching episodes. The purpose of the vignettes is to clarify each level of the continuum as they relate to oral language and to help teachers evaluate the oral language of their students. This evaluation will support student learning in oral language and move students along the continuum.

GUIDING QUESTIONS

- Where are my students on the broad developmental levels of the continuum in relation to oral language?
- Do my interactions with students have clear and focused objectives that ultimately move them through a learning continuum?

- Where are my students on the broad developmental levels of the continuum in relation to oral language?

- Do my interactions with students have clear and focused objectives that ultimately move them through a learning continuum?

---

1. The student will not converse about his or her work. However, he or she may gesture.

EXPLORING LEVELS OF PROFICIENCY IN STUDENTS' ORAL LANGUAGE

As in Student Work, Students' Oral Language can be categorized into different levels of proficiency. We found we could not effectively evaluate a student's work unless we also had the student tell us about the picture. As with the drawings or constructions, we found many commonalities among students' stories. Some students could not articulate what they had drawn. Others used one-word labels, and still others could put one and two sentence stories together. Some students changed their stories each time they talked about their pictures; others held steadfast. The following vignettes are examples of these different levels of students' oral language.

ORAL LANGUAGE AT LEVEL 1

The student will not converse about his or her work. However, he or she may gesture.

There are several reasons why students do not converse about their work. One may simply be that the child has not been engaged in—or lacks experience with—social conversations. Another may be that the child has language or cognitive delays that interfere with expressive or receptive communication. A third reason may be that his or her native language is different from the language used in the classroom. Mary is an example of a child in this situation. Notice as you read the first vignette how the teacher uses a non-English speaking student's picture to prepare for later work in oral language development.

Mary is a new student from China. According to language testing at the beginning of school, she speaks no English. She has been in school for four weeks. She spends much of her time in the classroom in limited interactions with other students or the teacher. Mary functions in the classroom by observing other students as they respond to the teacher's directions. As the other students begin to draw, Mary does too. She picks up the pink crayon and draws a face and a flower. To support Mary, the teacher arranges for frequent interactions. The teacher only waits a few minutes, giving Mary an opportunity to draw her picture, before going over to her. He points to the face and asks, "Is this you?" There is no response. The teacher points to the flower and says, "This is a pretty flower. Do you like flowers?" Still there is no verbal response from Mary, but she smiles. The teacher points to the flower, nodding yes, and says, "Yes, I think you do like flowers."

The teacher jots down a few monitoring notes about his interaction with Mary (see Figure 6.1). He wants to record this information so he can remember it later as he evaluates the interaction. He also wants documentation of his interactions with Mary between formal assessments. In writing anecdotal or monitoring notes, it is important to note the behaviors of the student as well as the action of the teacher in order to more accurately evaluate the interaction.

This teacher understands that children who are beginning to acquire a second language usually go through a silent period. The teacher understands the child's need for frequent verbal interactions during this receptive period. The purpose of these intentional interactions is to model the vocabulary, grammar, syntax, and subtleties of the new language. Therefore, the teacher must continue to engage Mary in frequent verbal interactions regardless of her current ability to respond in English. In doing so, he understands that he must use

- Where are my students on the broad developmental levels of the continuum in relation to oral language?

- Do my interactions with students have clear and focused objectives that ultimately move them through a learning continuum?

Name: *Mary*   **Date:** *10/01*

Activity/Center: *Picture drawing*

Current Student Work Level: *2*

Current Oral Language Level: *1*

Notes
Student: *Watched other students as they drew pictures; drew a face and a flower; did not talk about drawing*

Teacher: *Suggested face was Mary's and that she liked flowers*

Next Step: *Go over this story with Mary tomorrow; Try to elicit the story from Mary by looking at the picture and discussing it with her*

Figure 6.1: Monitoring Notes on Oral Language at Level 1

what she can do—her drawings and constructions—to make connections that will eventually lead to increased communicative competence in her new language. The teacher knows the power of helping Mary extend the thoughts expressed in her drawing through *his* language, because at this time she cannot.

ORAL LANGUAGE AT LEVEL 2

The student gives one word, a short phrase, or a simple sentence about his or her work through teacher questioning. However, the student may seem unsure and/or give different responses during continued conversation.

> 2. The student gives one word, a short phrase, or a simple sentence about his or her work through teacher questioning. However, the student may seem unsure and/or give different responses during continued conversation.

There are several reasons why students change their stories during conversation. One reason may be that they think the teacher's questions indicate that the teacher is not pleased with the first story offered. Another reason is that after telling a story to the teacher, the student has forgotten it. Students may also be unsure of how to represent part of the originally told story in their drawings. A fourth reason that students might change their stories is that they have patterned their story after another student's story. Here is an example of such a case. In the following vignette, notice how the teacher leads the student back to the original topic and does not allow him to change his story several times. Note as well, Johnny's upbeat behavior as he leaves the teaching episode.

The teacher sits at the table as students are preparing to draw their stories. During a discussion with the teacher, Johnny seems very clear about what his story will be for today. When asked, he says, "It's about me and Daddy going to get ice cream." The teacher says, "Draw the picture and I'll come back in a minute." The teacher then turns her atten-

- Where are my students on the broad developmental levels of the continuum in relation to oral language?

- Do my interactions with students have clear and focused objectives that ultimately move them through a learning continuum?

tion to other students who have been drawing. After taking dictation from those students, the teacher returns to Johnny who has completed his drawing. He has drawn a picture with two people containing some difficult-to-identify details. When asked to tell the teacher about the picture, he says, "This is me and Grandma playing ball."

Rather than allow him to wander in his topic choice, the teacher looks confused and says, "Are you telling your story or Mike's?" Mike, a boy sitting next to Johnny at the writing table, had just completed a similar story. "I thought you said this would be your story of you and Daddy going for ice cream." The teacher continues, "Did you change your mind?" The student says, "This is me and my friend playing ball." At this point the teacher decides that she needs to help Johnny stay on topic as he discusses his story and drawing. The teacher responds, "You told me that this would be the story of you and Daddy going for ice cream. You have drawn two people. One looks like you and the other looks like your Daddy." Pointing to the unidentifiable detail the teacher asks, "Is this the ice cream that Daddy bought for you?" Johnny nods and the teacher continues. "Let's make it look more like an ice cream cone so we can remember that this is your story about Daddy buying ice cream for you." Johnny and the teacher together, enhance the detail of the piece by drawing a triangle with a circle on top to represent the ice cream. Johnny takes the drawing and happily goes to share it with his friend who is reading books in the classroom library. He says, "Look what I did. I made the story of me and Daddy getting ice cream." Johnny's demeanor as he shares his story with his friend is evidence that he is proud of his accomplishment. Later that day, in order to document her interaction with Johnny, the teacher writes some notes about his story that captures what happened and will help her plan appropriate instruction for this student (see Figure 6.2).

Name: *Johnny* Date: *1/21*

Activity/Center: *Picture journal*

Current Student Work Level: *3*

Current Oral Language Level: *2*

Notes
Student: *Initial story before drawing-"Me and daddy going to get ice cream." Changed story after seeing another student's drawing-"This is grandma and me playing ball." Drew people and included some unidentifiable detail*

Teacher: *reminded Johnny about his original story; helped him draw ice cream details*

Next Step: *To help cement the story, talk about the detail he is going to put into his picture before he begins to work*

Figure 6.2: Documenting Oral Language at Level 2

- Where are my students on the broad developmental levels of the continuum in relation to oral language?

- Do my interactions with students have clear and focused objectives that ultimately move them through a learning continuum?

The teacher makes note of the student's initial story because she understands that at this level students are often impulsive and need support in staying on topic and remembering their story. Had his teacher allowed Johnny to change his story several times, what message would she have sent about the constancy of the picture or print? How would he have viewed the connection between the picture and story?

The teacher understands that her students need to know that what they think, feel, or experience can be represented on paper. The student must also know that once a picture is drawn or a construction is made, that the story will remain the same each time it is revisited. This thinking is the foundation of understanding the "constancy of print"-the idea that once a story is on paper the topic or idea does not change from reading to reading.

ORAL LANGUAGE AT LEVEL 3

The student gives one word, short phrases, or a simple sentence about his or her work. The language remains constant during the conversation and over time.

At Level 3, as in Level 2, the oral language is still relatively simple. The contrast between the two levels is that students at Level 3 are not as likely to wander in their conversation about their drawing or construction. They are more confident about their work as well as their words or story, and they can remember it over an extended period of time. Because making meaning is such an important part of the interaction between this student and teacher, notice how hard they work at communicating and understanding the story.

> 3. The student gives one word, short phrases, or a simple sentence about his or her work. The language remains constant during the conversation and over time.

Carlos, a Spanish-speaking student who is learning English, has made steady progress in his acquisition of English vocabulary and is at Level 3 on the continuum in his oral language development. His teacher knows that he has gone from appearing unsure about his story to displaying more confidence in communicating his story. During a teaching episode with Carlos, the teacher talks to him about his picture. When Carlos shows the teacher his drawing, he looks very pleased and says, "Daddy **buy**." The teacher asks, "Where's Daddy?" Carlos looks a bit unsure and points to a table-like object in his picture. Now the teacher is confused and asks, "What is that? What did you draw?" Carlos repeats, "Daddy buy—*tienda* (store)." Now the teacher points to a table in the classroom and says, "Table? Did your Daddy buy the table at the store?" Carlos shakes his head no. At this point it is obvious that Carlos is very sure of what he wants to say but lacks the oral language to express his story in English. The teacher tries one more time to understand. Pointing to the picture, she asks, "What did Daddy buy? What is that?" Carlos seems to think for a moment, stands, and then begins to jump up and down with his arms extended out. The teacher excitedly says, "A trampoline? Did your Daddy buy a trampoline for you?" Carlos grins from ear-to-ear and says, "*Sí!*-tram-pa-lin." The teacher says "Yes, trampoline" and writes trampoline next to Carlos' picture. Now the teacher points to the picture and repeats the word. Carlos smiles again and says, "Trampoline." Carlos and the teacher are both pleased with the results of their hard work. The teacher documents her experience with Carlos (Figure 6.3).

- Where are my students on the broad developmental levels of the continuum in relation to oral language?

- Do my interactions with students have clear and focused objectives that ultimately move them through a learning continuum?

Name: *Carlos*   **Date:** *11/19*

Activity/Center: *Picture journal*

Current Student Work Level: *3*

Current Oral Language Level: *3*

Notes
Student: *Initial story "Daddy buy." Drew a table-like structure; didn't have the English vocabulary to explain; acted out word*

Teacher: *guessed word trampoline; Labeled picture*

Next Step: *Go over previous stories; needs lots of discussion after initial drawing*

Figure 6.3: Monitoring Notes on an English Language Learner

The teacher notes her support of vocabulary development. She knows that if an English as a Second Language (ESL) student is to develop in his oral language, his pictures or constructions are a good source of teaching. She also makes sure she labels the picture to ensure they both remember the new vocabulary over time.

The teacher knows that the time it takes to understand students' messages is time well spent, because students at this level are coming to understand more consistently that their stories should not change dramatically from telling to telling. The teacher understands that for an ESL student to communicate his story he must have the language that represents the critical details of that story. ESL students know much more than they are able to articulate in English. The teacher needs to support them by helping them find the English words that correspond to the picture or the story. When the teacher provides this type of encouragement and support in finding the right words, the students know their work is valued and are further motivated to convey their messages.

ORAL LANGUAGE AT LEVEL 4

The student is able to tell a story about his or her work through teacher questioning.

> 4. The student is able to tell a story about his or her work through teacher questioning.

At Level 4, the student readily tells a story that goes beyond the simple sentence of Level 3. This story is detailed, but may be missing some important parts and/or it may not be in sequential order. Through questioning, the teacher works at developing the story by helping the student fill in missing parts and/or sequence events. Notice how the teacher probes to uncover the "real" story from what the student first shared and how this brings out the child's voice in the story.

- Where are my students on the broad developmental levels of the continuum in relation to oral language?

- Do my interactions with students have clear and focused objectives that ultimately move them through a learning continuum?

During breakfast the teacher notices a small cut beneath Jeremy's nose. The teacher points to his nose and asks, "What happened?" Jeremy begins to tell about playing a game with his brother, Reggie. He makes no mention of his hurt nose or of any other trouble. The teacher inquires, "Did you hurt your nose while you were playing with Reggie?" Jeremy responds, "Granny got mad." "Well, why did Granny get mad?" "'Cause I cried." he said. "Did you cry because your nose was hurt?" "Yeah, Reggie swinged his belt." The teacher nods her head knowingly and says, "I think that would make a great story to draw a picture about. Don't you?" Jeremy agrees.

After breakfast, the teacher reminds Jeremy about the story he told earlier and sends him to the writing center. Jeremy begins to sketch the story he told since he already knows exactly what it will be about. As the teacher roves around the room to monitor and teach other children, she notices that Jeremy has finished with his drawing and is talking to another student at the writing center. As she sits down to talk with him about his picture, she notices that he has all the important parts of the story represented in his drawing-himself, Reggie holding the belt, and Granny. He even has the detail of the blood under his nose.

The teacher understands that during conversation she can monitor for and teach skills such as having a focus, using supporting detail, and organizing one's thoughts (Figure 6.4). This will support oral language development as well as later reading and writing instruction and learning.

Because the teacher knows where Jeremy is in his oral language in relation to the continuum, she will write the story that he dictates to her. The teacher asks Jeremy to talk about his picture. She helps him

Name: *Jeremy*   Date: *2/3*

Activity/Center: *Picture journal*

Current Student Work Level: *4*

Current Oral Language Level: *4*

Notes
Student: *Started with the end of his story first—"Granny got mad"*

Teacher: *Talked with Jeremy about his cut; walked through the details of his story*

Next Step: *Talk with Jeremy before he draws to help him sequence his story.*

Figure 6.4: Monitoring Focus, Detail, and Organization of Oral Language

- Where are my students on the broad developmental levels of the continuum in relation to oral language?

- Do my interactions with students have clear and focused objectives that ultimately move them through a learning continuum?

sequence the story by asking questions such as, "What happened before your nose got hurt?" This helps him think about the beginning of his story. As Jeremy's story unfolds through more conversation, the sequence becomes more evident. Jeremy ends his story with Granny entering the room and asking, "Reginald, do you need me to give you a whuppin'?" Because the teacher knows that Granny's "bark is worse than her bite," the teacher laughs and Jeremy joins in. By using Granny's admonishment as the dictated story, the writer's voice is captured for all to share.

The teacher understands that if she knows the continuum objectives for her students, teaching can occur whenever and wherever she and students are together. With students at Level 4 on the oral language section of the continuum, the teacher knows that the story can be discussed prior to the drawing of the picture or the construction activity. Jeremy now remembers his stories over time because his teacher's instruction focuses on his oral language and his attention to details, both of which develop the stories he has to tell. She also understands that there is usually more to a child's story than what he or she articulates at first. This teacher identifies the challenges for her students by listening to what they say, watching what they do, and framing questions that develop the sequence and/or completeness of the story. By developing the whole story—and subsequently the "voice" of the child—the teacher understands the importance of engaging the child in natural conversation. This carefully engineered and intentional conversation results in getting the real story the child has to tell but still may have trouble articulating. The teacher also understands that most of a child's story will be expressed through oral language, and that she needs to take dictation only on the most important part of the story. It is the final part of Jeremy's story that she thinks will help him recall the entire story orally.

ORAL LANGUAGE AT LEVEL 5

5. The student is able to tell a simple story about his or her work with little or no teacher support.

The student is able to tell a simple story about his or her work with little or no teacher support.

At Level 5 the oral stories are well developed, and the students need little support from the teacher. The stories are usually complete and well organized. Often, these stories have a strong beginning, middle, and end. The focus during this time is to have students tell stories about their work regardless of where the work occurs in the classroom, such as the block, clay, dramatic play, puppets, or flannel board areas. Even though teaching at centers should occur with children at any level of the continuum, it is especially important at Level 5. Students at this level have strong abilities to tell well-developed stories, but need to be encouraged to recognize that stories can come from their center activities throughout the room. Ultimately, they should be able to find a story in any life experience. Notice, as you read the following vignette, the conversation of the students at the center and how the teacher uses that conversation to extend one student's learning at this higher level.

Several children are playing in the dramatic play area of the classroom, which currently is set up to represent a doctor's office. The teacher joins the group just as they are discussing the fact that the baby doll is sick. The teacher questions, "Should we call the doctor over so we can get some medicine for the baby?" This steers the conversation to talk of doctor appointments. As the children share stories of previous doctor's visits, Katie turns her attention to the teacher and says, "One time my mommy went to the doctor, and he said she had a baby in her tummy, and the baby was *me!*"

Later in the morning when Katie works at the writing center, she says, "I don't know what story to tell about." Remembering the

- Where are my students on the broad developmental levels of the continuum in relation to oral language?

- Do my interactions with students have clear and focused objectives that ultimately move them through a learning continuum?

earlier interaction in the dramatic play area, the teacher suggests, "You could write the story about the time your mommy was having you. That would make an interesting story, wouldn't it?" Katie agrees and begins to draw her picture.

Before Katie begins, the teacher asks her to tell the story one more time. While Katie is drawing, the teacher says, "I see your mom, I see you as the baby inside her tummy (a baby inside a big circle in the middle of a stick figure), and you both have smiles on your faces. Why are you smiling?" Katie says with a big grin on her face now, "Because she was having *me*!" The teacher says, "Oh yes, that's what you said at the end of your story." The teacher writes, "Mommy went to the doctor because she was having me." Then the teacher asks, "Why don't you write the word 'me' there (pointing to the baby in the mother's stomach) and 'mom' there (pointing to the mother in the picture)?" Later the teacher writes a few notes on his interactions with Katie (Figure 6.5).

Katie's oral language and pictures are very detailed. Her teacher understands the need for development in these areas in order for his students to be successful as they move from picture journals to writing journals, where the focus moves from pictures to sound/letter correspondence.

Even though the teacher knows that students at Level 5 on the oral language section of the continuum are secure in their story and need little, if any, support to tell it, he knows that he may need to check and reinforce the story structure with these students. He also understands that the natural conversations within his classroom centers provide excellent opportunities for him to help students select topics

Name: *Katie*   Date: *5/11*

Activity/Center: *Picture journal*

Current Student Work Level: 5

Current Oral Language Level: 5

Notes
Student: *After reminding of earlier topic, Katie remembers her story almost verbatim; very detailed drawing*

Teacher: *Reminded Katie of story when she was born; had her label "mom" and "me" in her picture*

Next Step: *Needs to be in a writing journal where she can focus on sound/letter correspondence*

Figure 6.5: Monitoring Notes Showing a Student Ready to Move to the Next Step

- Where are my students on the broad developmental levels of the continuum in relation to oral language?

- Do my interactions with students have clear and focused objectives that ultimately move them through a learning continuum?

and/or expand ideas for their stories. He knows too that conversation while the students work can help keep the picture as focused as the story. This teacher understands that oral language and a student's work are hard to separate. At Level 5 the teacher may ask the child to label what she can *while* the child is telling the story. Labeling serves as another anchor for the child to remember and retell the story, as well as an example that words *and* pictures hold meaning.

Just as in Chapter 5, these teaching vignettes illustrate the idea that all of the teacher's interactions should move students along the learning continuum. In this chapter the focus was on supporting students in their oral language development. Even though the learning may not be noticeably evident at the point of teaching, over time and with focused instruction students will progress through the Student's Oral Language levels of the continuum. The following chapter deals with the use of specific objectives, which serve as a vehicle to move students through the levels of the continuum.

Chapter 7   Choosing Teaching Objectives

The Teaching Objectives section of the **Early Literacy Continuum** helps teachers organize and manage the objectives used for teaching in natural and developmentally appropriate ways. This section plays an integral part in utilizing the continuum. While the Student's Work and Student's Oral Language sections of the continuum deal with the *assessment* of the speaker, reader, and writer, the Teaching Objectives section deals with the objectives for *teaching* the student as the speaker, reader, and writer.

GUIDING QUESTIONS

- How are my current teaching objectives organized for teaching?
- How do I decide which teaching methods are the best for my students?

CONNECTING ASSESSMENT AND TEACHING

When teachers use the continuum as an assessment tool, the focus is on the student in relation to the broad developmental levels of Student's Work and Student's Oral Language (see Chapter 8 for a completed continuum example). These levels offer teachers a way to monitor each of their student's growth over time and provide them with a starting point for instruction with each student. The levels of Student's Work and Student's Oral Language are too broad to focus the teaching needed if students are to grow in their literacy development. The Teaching Objectives section of the continuum is the bridge that connects the developmental levels of Student's Work and Student's Oral Language and the act of teaching. To be effective,

- How are my current teaching objectives organized for teaching?

- How do I decide which teaching methods are the best for my students?

teaching should be based on assessments that lead to the selection and use of a specific and focused objective. The Teaching Objectives section is where those specific and focused objectives can be found (see Chapter 8 for a completed Teaching Objectives section of the continuum).

FOCUSED TEACHING THROUGH CONVERSATION

The Teaching Objectives section of the continuum is separated into three distinct boxes. The top box focuses on developing conversation about the student's work and adding details to that work. Objectives from this box primarily support the teaching that occurs for students at Levels 1 and 2, but may also be used at Level 3 of both Student's Work and Student's Oral Language. The objectives within the first box guide the conversation and lead the student to add details based on one of these objectives. At this level the teacher does not take dictation but may label the objects within the picture. Interactions of this nature are highly supportive of children at these initial levels and facilitate the movement of the child from one level to the next. Because these interactions are oral, it is critical that the teacher keep anecdotal notes of the teacher/student interaction during that teaching episode.

FOCUSED TEACHING THROUGH DICTATION

The middle box of the Teaching Objectives section of the continuum focuses on taking dictation. Objectives contained within this section primarily support Levels 3 and 4 of Student's Work and Student's Oral Language portions of the continuum. At these levels dictation is the vehicle teachers use to extend students' oral language and the adding of detail to the student work. Teachers may need to use dictation at Level 5 as well, depending on the child. Teacher interactions with students at Levels 3 and 4 should always result in the teacher recording the student's dictated story. At these levels dictation is taken because the student is coming to understand that stories can be written down and remain constant when revisited. When taking dictation, teachers need to also consider periodically revisiting objectives from the top box.

FOCUSED TEACHING THROUGH STUDENT WRITING

As students move into Levels 4 and 5 they need to be encouraged to add writing to their work. It may initially take the form of labels within the picture, but later students should be encouraged to write their story at the bottom of the picture; much in the way they have seen the teacher take dictation. The student's writing may include controlled scribbling, formation of mock letters, random strings, and/or semi-phonetic attempts at spelling. Whatever the child produces should be praised to encourage his or her continued approximations. It is approximations such as these that give insight into the student's current writing skills and provide the teacher with the information needed for the child's next learning steps.

The last box of the Teaching Objectives section contains objectives that are specific to the students' recording of their own stories. This last box relates only to Level 5 on the continuum because work at this level closely resembles the writing that is most often seen in kindergarten. It is here that the primary emphasis begins to shift from the teacher's role of taking dictation to the students' role of recording their own messages. Because of this shift, student control of oral language and adding detail must be well in place. The

- How are my current teaching objectives organized for teaching?

- How do I decide which teaching methods are the best for my students?

stronger the students' control of oral language and adding detail the more able the students will be to record their own messages. Many prekindergarten students may not reach this level because they have not yet achieved the developmental capability for the skills involved in the third box of the Teaching Objectives section: identifying letters, accurate letter formation, some understanding of letter/sound correspondences, basic print conventions, and an association between spoken and written word by following print as it is read. To learn more about teaching students who have exceeded Level 5 skills in both Student's Work and Student's Oral Language on the **Early Literacy Continuum,** we recommend *The Kindergarten Book: A Guide to Literacy Instruction,* by Marilyn Duncan (2005); *A Book Is a Present: Selecting Text for Intentional Teaching* by Margaret E. Mooney (2004a), and *Reading for Life: The Learner as a Reader* (1997) and *Dancing with the Pen: The Learner as a Writer* (1992), both by the New Zealand Ministry of Education.

ORGANIZING THE TEACHING OBJECTIVES

The **Early Literacy Continuum** is not only a convenient tool to assess student learning but it is also an effective way to support teaching. When used properly the Teaching Objectives section of the continuum organizes a district's or state's objectives around teaching methods or approaches. It matches up these teaching methods to the developmental levels of Student's Oral Language and Student's Work. Thus the objectives become the teaching vehicle or the focus to move the students through the development levels of Student's Oral Language and Student's Work.

The following chapter, Collecting and Organizing the Data, demonstrates how two districts organized their prekindergarten objectives by using the Teaching Objectives section of the **Early Literacy Continuum** and how they are working to align their prekindergarten objectives to the bigger picture of the entire district.

Chapter 8

Collecting and Organizing the Data

The **Early Literacy Continuum** is a convenient and effective way to give structure to a district's or state's prekindergarten or kindergarten objectives within an organized and developmental framework. The continuum assists teachers and curriculum developers as they work to meet objectives in all areas of curriculum, and as they align the prekindergarten or kindergarten objectives to the bigger picture of the entire district. This chapter looks at two urban districts and how they used the **Early Literacy Continuum** to help organize to assess and teach their prekindergarten students.

GUIDING QUESTION

- What can I do with the information I am gathering on my students?

The **Early Literacy Continuum** resulted from a two-year collaboration between the authors when they worked together in Arlington, Texas. Presently, the Arlington District is in its fourth year of using the continuum to guide literacy instruction for prekindergarten students. Since that beginning work in Arlington, Cartwright School District in Phoenix, Arizona has also begun to use the continuum. Note how the districts have each created their own unique reporting instruments. One district is actively using the assessment results to determine the mean, median, and mode scores for each reporting period as a vehicle for student achievement as well as to plan professional development for its teachers. The other district is establishing benchmarks for student work at each reporting period.

• What can I do with the information I am gathering on my students?

The following stories show how these districts in different states have each embraced the use of the continuum, and have custom tailored the **Early Literacy Continuum's** content and reporting procedures to meet their district and state guidelines.

ENHANCING A PREKINDERGARTEN PROGRAM IN TEXAS

Arlington Independent School District (AISD) is an urban school district in the Dallas/Fort Worth metroplex of Texas. AISD is the eighth largest district in the state and sixty-sixth largest in the nation. The district has a total student population of approximately 61,000 of which 3,000 are prekindergarten students. The district population is over 58 percent nonwhite. More than 150 teachers and assistants serve the prekindergarten students in 44 schools.

Objectives from the *State of Texas Commissioner's Guidelines for Prekindergarten* were used to customize the **Early Literacy Continuum** for use in Arlington. Figure 8.1 shows how the continuum was adapted and completed by AISD. These objectives were primarily taken from the Language and Early Literacy portion of the Texas guidelines. However, objectives from all of the curriculum areas (Language and Literacy, Mathematics, Social and Emotional Development, Physical Development) were also considered.

The AISD prekindergarten department currently supplies the **Early Literacy Continuum** to all prekindergarten teachers and expects all students to be assessed on the continuum three times a year. The results of these assessments are placed in a student portfolio that also includes additional literacy related assessments, recorded on a Class Summary Sheet, and turned in to the prekindergarten lead

Arlington Independent School District Prekindergarten Writing Samples

(scored using the Early Literacy Continuum below)

(dated writing samples attached)

Student Name: _____

Teacher Name: _____

School Year: _____

School: _____

Student's Oral Language
(in the language of instruction)

1. The student will not converse about his or her work. However, he or she may gesture.

2. The student gives one word, a short phrase, or a simple sentence about his or her work through teacher questioning. However, the student may seem unsure and/or give different responses during continued conversation.

3. The student gives one word, short phrases, or a simple sentence about his or her work. The story remains constant during continued conversation.

4. The student is able to tell a story about his or her work through teacher questioning.

5. The student is able to tell a simple story about his or her work with little or no teacher support.

Teaching Objectives*

The student will add detail to his or her work through:
- engaging in conversation (staying on topic and taking turns).
- identifying character(s) and/or events of a story.
- beginning to retell some sequence of events in stories.
- asking questions and making comments about own work.
- telling a simple narrative, focusing on favorite or most memorable part.
- engaging in various forms of nonverbal communication with those who do not speak his or her home language (ESL).
- using single words and simple phrases to communicate meaning.
- attempting to use new vocabulary and grammar in speech (ESL).

As the student's work and language progresses, the student will:
- Begin to dictate words, phrases, or sentences for recording on paper.

As the student's "writing" progresses, he or she will use a draft book to:
- attempt to write messages in a variety of forms as part of a playful activity.
- use known letters and approximations of letters to represent written language.
- attempt to connect the sounds in a word with its letter forms.
- understand that writing is used to communicate ideas and information.
- understand that illustrations carry meaning but cannot be read.
- begin to understand some basic print conventions.
- begin to recognize the association between spoken and written words by following print as it is read.

Student's Work

1. The student's work consists of scribbles, random shapes, or exploration of materials. It is not recognizable.

2. The student's work is only recognizable when the student talks about it.

3. The student's work is recognizable, but lacks important detail that is critical to the story.

4. The student's work contains important detail that is critical to story, but lacks "writing."

5. The student's work contains important detail that is critical to the story, and includes "writing."

*State of Texas Commissioner's Guidelines for PreKindergarten Curriculum

Use #s 1-5 from above Continuum	Beginning Score	Middle Score	End Score
Language			
Product			

June 2004 *Required documentation for Prekindergarten Portfolio*

Figure 8.1: Arlington Independent School District Adaptation of the Early Literacy Continuum

teacher. The results on the Class Summary Sheets provide the following information:

- evidence of growth over time for individual students
- information needed for the prekindergarten lead teacher to plan staff development and individual teacher support
- statistics that set the benchmarks for expected student progress at specified reporting periods.

Figure 8.2 shows a partially completed sample class summary sheet that documents students' growth over the school year using the Early Literacy Continuum scoring levels for Student Work (Prod.) and Oral Language (Lang.). A blank form appears in Appendix A.

ENHANCING A PREKINDERGARTEN PROGRAM IN ARIZONA

Cartwright School District is an urban school district in the Phoenix metropolitan area. The district has a population of roughly 21,000 elementary and middle school students, plus over 700 prekindergarten students. Over 88 percent of those prekindergarten students come from Spanish-speaking homes. The prekindergarten campus houses both the district prekindergarten as well as Head Start programs. There are 26 teachers on Cartwright's preschool campus.

Many of the objectives from the Arizona Early Childhood Education Standards were used to modify the **Early Literacy Continuum** for Cartwright preschool's needs. Many of these objectives were taken from the Language and Early Literacy portion of the state's standards. However, when deciding which objectives would be used for the development of the Teaching Objectives portion of the continu-

Prekindergarten Assessment Summary Sheet

Teacher: _____ **AM or PM**

School: _____ **School Year:** _____

Student's Name	Letter Identification (English 52) (Spanish 61)									Writing Sample						Phonological Awareness (6 items per concept)									Print Awareness		
	Letter Name			Letter Sound			Word			Prod. (5 levels)			Lang. (5 levels)			Beginning Sound			Rhyming Words			Clap Syllables			(11 Concepts)		
	Beg.	Mid.	End	Beg.	Mid.	End	Beg.	Mid.	End	Beg.	Mid.	End	Beg.	Mid.	End	Beg.	Mid.	End	Beg.	Mid.	End	Beg.	Mid.	End	Beg.	Mid.	End
*										1	2	4	1	3	3												
										1	4	5	2	3	4												
										2	2	3	2	3	4												
										1	2	4	2	3	4												
										2	4	5	1	3	4												
										1	3	4	1	2	3												
										2	2	3	2	2	4												
										3	4	5	2	5	5												
										3	3	5	1	3	4												
										1	3	5	3	4	5												
										3	3	4	3	4	5												
										1	2	3	2	2	4												
										1	4	5	2	4	5												
										2	2	3	2	3	4												
										1	3	5	1	3	3												

To be turned in to the principal at the end of the school year.

Adapted from Arlington ISD, Arlington, Texas, June 2004.

*Names removed to ensure confidentiality.

Figure 8.2: Partially Completed Class Summary Sheet

um, Cartwright's Prekindergarten Curriculum Team considered all the objectives from each curriculum area (Language and Literacy, Mathematics, Social and Emotional Development, Physical Development). Because this prekindergarten school campus had recently merged with Head Start, objectives from the Head Start Guidelines were also considered for the Cartwright adaptation of the **Early Literacy Continuum.** The objectives chosen by Cartwright's Prekindergarten Curriculum Team were divided into three groups. Each group represents one of the three boxes of the Teaching Objectives section on the continuum (see Figure 8.3). The first box contains those objectives that support literacy teaching through oral language. The second box houses the objectives that support the understanding that print, as well as pictures, contain the message. Those objectives support teaching through dictation. The third box contains objectives for students who are beginning to write their own messages. Many of the objectives in this box support students who are coming to understand letter/sound connections. Because of the standards contained in their state frameworks, most of the objectives the Prekindergarten Curriculum Team developed for use in the continuum fit within the first two boxes. There were few objectives that seemed to fit into the third box of the Teaching Objectives section of the **Early Literacy Continuum.**

The curriculum team needed to look at other sources for the objectives in the third box of the **Teaching Objectives** section. In order to develop instructional continuity throughout the district, they decided that the kindergarten objectives were appropriate for the third box. It made sense that if students had successfully moved through the first two boxes of the Teaching Objectives section on Cartwright's **Early Literacy Continuum** or had come into

Early Literacy Continuum

Level of Student's Work	Teaching Objectives	Level of Student's Oral Language[1] (in the language of instruction)
1. The student's work consists of scribbles, random shapes, or exploration of materials. It is not recognizable.	**Through conversation and by the student adding on to his/her work, the student will be able to:** • stay on topic. • identify character(s) and/or event(s) of a story. • retell some sequence of events. • make connections to self, others, and/or environment. • use both real and make-believe situations. • answer questions. • ask questions and make comments on work. • apply knowledge/experiences to new areas (drawing, painting, blocks, housekeeping, etc.)	1. The student will not converse about his or her work. However, he or she may gesture.
2. The student's work is only recognizable when the student talks about it.		2. The student gives one word, a short phrase, or a simple sentence about his or her work through teacher questioning. However, the student may seem unsure and/or give different responses during continued conversation.
3. The student's work is recognizable, but lacks important detail that is critical to the story.	**The student will add on to his/her own work and will be able to:** • tell a simple story, focusing on favorite or most important part. (Teacher will take dictation.)	3. The student gives one word, short phrases, or a simple sentence about his or her work. The language remains constant during the conversation and over time.
4. The student's work contains important detail that is critical to the story, but lacks "writing."		4. The student is able to tell a story about his or her work through teacher questioning.
5. The student's work contains important detail that is critical to the story and includes "writing."	**In the student's journal or writing book, the student will be able to:** • understand that the illustration holds most of the meaning when reading text. • use letter/letter-like symbols to represent writing. • understand that writing has a purpose. • recognize the connection between the spoken and written word. • identify letters. • connect sounds to their letters. • understand some concepts about print.	5. The student is able to tell a simple story about his or her work with little or no teacher support.

[1]In ELL/ESL and bilingual classrooms, dictation is taken in the language of instruction. For example, in a Spanish bilingual classroom, the language of instruction is Spanish. In any ELL/ESL classroom, the language of instruction is English.

Figure 8.3: Cartwright School District's Adaptation of the Continuum

prekindergarten already beyond the first two boxes; they would need more advanced writing and reading instruction. This third box would resemble the district's current kindergarten program, but the students would remain in an age-appropriate prekindergarten classroom. Figure 8.3 shows how this district tailored the continuum to help fulfill their state and Head Start literacy needs.

The Cartwright's Preschool Curriculum Team gave their finished version of the **Early Literacy Continuum** to all prekindergarten teachers and set the expectation that *all* students would be formally assessed four times a year. (See Cartwright School District's Assessment Guide in Appendix B; Scoring Considerations in Appendix C; Individual Student Recording Sheet in Appendix D; and Classroom Summary Sheet in Appendix E.) The four assigned dates help teachers plan for assessing and evaluating their students. On those dates, teachers attach students' evaluated drawings and dictations to the Individual Student Recording Sheets and turn them in to the principal. The teachers also turn in their Classroom Summary Sheet, displaying the data for their classes as a whole. The school's leadership team then organizes and analyzes the data, calculating the mean, median, and mode scores.

Calculating the mean (average) of a class helps the teacher determine where a particular child is in relation to the class. Mean scores can also help schools set benchmarks at different times of the year. This can be a support for determining whether or not a student is making adequate progress in relation to the school population, and it can aid the teacher or school in making decisions about the need to offer additional teaching support. These mean scores can be graphed to give a visual representation of student achievement, as shown in Figures 8.4 and 8.5.

STUDENT WORK

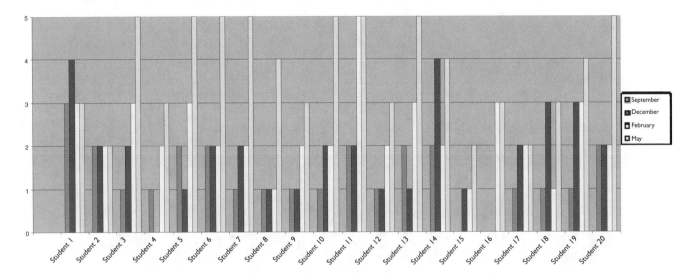

Figure 8.4: Achievement in Student Work in a Classroom Using the Early Literacy Continuum

The median scores are similar to mean scores in that they give the teacher an average score, but mean scores are calculated differently. Median scores are derived by listing the scores by their values, highest to lowest or lowest to highest, and then selecting the middle-most score. This score can be very useful to teachers because it reflects a number that relates directly to the scores being calculated from the continuum. The mean scores will often have a score that is not exactly represented by numbers that are on the **Early Literacy Continuum.** For example, the scores on the continuum are represented by the whole numbers one through five but mean scores could result in a number such as a 4.5.

Oral Language

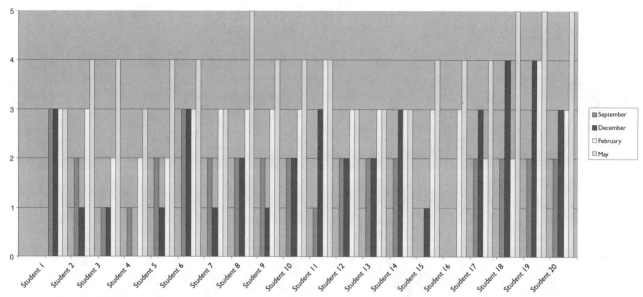

Figure 8.5: Student Oral Language Achievement in a Classroom Using the Early Literacy Continuum

Mode scores relate the most frequently occurring number in a series of numbers. This score is helpful to teachers or districts in that it creates a norm for comparing student achievement from classroom to classroom. This type of score supports the teacher, school, or district in the analysis of how to raise student achievement levels.

These results are shared with the full leadership team, district office, and teachers. The implications for using results such as these are threefold. First, teachers use the results to reflect on their teaching as it compares to the school as a whole. Secondly, the results support the school's leadership team to determine what kind of professional development the teachers need. Thirdly, the results document student growth over time for administrators, parents, and teachers.

Figures 8.4 and 8.5 show growth over time for one prekindergarten class. Note that all children but one in the Oral Language graph and two students in Student Work made gains across the year. By looking at the results of this teacher's classroom data in graph form, it is easy to see individual students who have made lots of progress, individual students who have "flatlined," and each individual student's peaks and valleys of learning. Questions teachers and administrators can ask as they analyze the graph may include:

- Why did certain students make such strong growth?
- Why did some students not make any growth?
- Why did some students seem to go backwards?

The graph can also show teachers trends for the whole class, as well as growth benchmarks for students at particular times of the year. Questions that center on the whole group may include:

- What does the average student look like at this time of year?
- What kinds of skills should I be teaching to the whole group right now?

CAUSE FOR CHANGE

As one prekindergarten teacher who uses the continuum puts it, "In the past, my teaching of reading and writing in prekindergarten was not only not focused, but I lacked the understandings I needed to even know why an activity was being done and what the objective was. I had a filing cabinet of literacy activities and a classroom full of children who did those activities whether they needed work on those skills or not. To put it frankly, I couldn't have told you what each child needed because I didn't know. . . .That is exactly what the Early Literacy Continuum has done for me. I have been brought to a whole new world of knowing my students."

Because of the **Early Literacy Continuum,** districts too "have been brought to a whole new world of knowing their students" As shown in this chapter, two districts have made major shifts in their approach to teaching and learning for their students, as well as how they gather and record student growth. More recently, because of the continuum, another district has begun to look at how to assess their prekindergarten students. They are questioning if the current assessment system they use is developmentally appropriate for prekindergarten children or if it will give them the specific information needed in order to improve learning for each student. For example:

- Are the assessments we currently use developmentally appropriate for our prekindergarten (or kindergarten) students?
- Are we getting the results we want in prekindergarten (or kindergarten) literacy?
- What does prekindergarten (or kindergarten) literacy look like?
- How are the results of these assessments affecting the teaching in our prekindergarten (or kindergarten) classrooms?

Many teachers and districts need to develop their understandings to know why an activity (or assessment) is used. Challenging questions need to be asked of—and answered by—teachers, parents, and administrators to make sure the youngest of our students are getting an education that is developmentally appropriate and based on evidence and research—an education that will provide those students with the skills they need to be successful now and in later school years.

APPENDICES

Appendix A

Prekindergarten Assessment Summary Sheet

Teacher: _____ **AM or PM**
School: _____ **School Year:** _____

Student's Name	Letter Identification (English 52) (Spanish 61)									Writing Sample						Phonological Awareness (6 items per concept)									Print Awareness		
	Letter Name			Letter Sound			Word			Prod. (5 levels)			Lang. (5 levels)			Beginning Sound			Rhyming Words			Clap Syllables			(11 Concepts)		
	Beg.	Mid.	End	Beg.	Mid.	End	Beg.	Mid.	End	Beg.	Mid.	End	Beg.	Mid.	End	Beg.	Mid.	End	Beg.	Mid.	End	Beg.	Mid.	End	Beg.	Mid.	End

To be turned in to the principal at the end of the school year.
Adapted from Arlington ISD, Arlington, Texas, June 2004.

*Names removed to ensure confidentiality.

Appendix B

The Early Literacy Continuum

Assessment Guide

1. Ask students to make a picture with materials that they are already familiar with using. For example: If the student has not used watercolors in the past, do *not* give him or her watercolors for the first time when you ask him/her to draw this picture.

2. Do *not* prompt the student about the work that is being completed. Questions are prompts. For example: Do *not* ask: "Where is your mommy in the picture?" or "What about your hair?"

3. When the student has completed the drawing say, "Tell me about your picture."

4. Write down the student's response to your request.

5. Read the student's response back to the student and ask: "Is there anything else that you want to add to your picture?"

6. If the student responds, allow the student to include more details and add the student's additional words to what you previously wrote. Sometimes after hearing their own words read back to them, students will decide that they wish to add more details to the picture and/or the explanation. *Never* push the student to do so; simply ask the question as given in #5.

7. The actual Early Literacy Continuum Individual Student Recording Sheet that you complete will be placed in each student's file with the student work sample the assessment is based upon.

8. The student's scores will be recorded on The Early Literacy Continuum Classroom Summary Sheet. It is this sheet that will be turned in to the district.

Adapted from Cartwright Preschool, Phoenix, Arizona, 2003.

Appendix C

The Early Literacy Continuum

Scoring Considerations

Student's Work:

1. Be objective when scoring the work sample. The score given will *not* be used to determine the effectiveness or the abilities of the teacher. The score is used *only* to measure children's progress over time.

2. Sometimes you may find that you have difficulty choosing between one score and the next higher number. When this occurs, *always* choose the lower number.

3. Even when the student draws shapes that are recognizable, if you are unable to figure out the purpose for the objects without an explanation, then the score is a 1.

4. Sometimes it really helps to confer with a colleague, especially one who has knowledge of the student. Often through this discussion you are able to form conclusions that you might not come to on your own.

Oral Language:

1. The assessment is designed to measure oral language development in English. If the student describes his or her drawing in Spanish, those words may be recorded in Spanish. The student is then asked to describe his or her drawing in English. Those words are recorded as well. The teacher will plan for individualization based upon the student's response or responses.

2. It is best practice to write an observation recording the student's words that were given in Spanish because although you won't use the Spanish words in this assessment, you certainly will use the student's details in your planning for individualization and on the developmental continuum.

3. As in the case of the work sample, when in doubt between two scores, *always* choose the lower score.

4. As in the case of the work sample, do not prompt the student or press for more details. Simply offer the opportunity to add details. If the student declines, end the activity and score based upon what has been provided.

Adapted from Cartwright Preschool, Phoenix, Arizona, 2003.

Appendix D

The Early Literacy Continuum

Individual Student Recording Sheet

Child's

Name: _____   Teacher: _____

Date of Birth: _____   Room # & Session: _____

Child's Primary Language: _____   Assessment Date: _____

Level of Student's Work

After applying the assessment guide considerations, please circle one description from the list below that best describes the work produced by the student in the assessment work sample.

1. The student's work consists of scribbles, random shapes, or exploration of materials. It is not recognizable.

2. The student's work is only recognizable when the student talks about it.

3. The student's work is recognizable, but it lacks detail that would differentiate one piece from another.

4. The student's work has many details.

5. The student's work has many details, and it includes writing.

Level of Student's Oral Language

After applying the assessment guide considerations, please circle one description from the list below that best describes the language produced by the student to describe the assessment work sample.

1. The student will not converse about his or her work. Student may gesture.

2. The student gives one word, short phrase, or simple sentence about his or her work through teacher questioning. At this level, the student may seem unsure and/or give different responses during conversation.

3. The student gives one-word labels, short phrases, or simple sentence about his or her work, and remains constant during conversation.

4. The student is able to tell a simple story about his or her work through teacher questioning.

5. The student tells a story about his or her work.

Continuum language © 2005 by Deborah K. Freeman and David M. Matteson. Adapted by Cartwright Preschool, Phoenix, Arizona, 2003.

Appendix E

The Early Literacy Continuum
*Classroom Summary Sheet**

Teacher:_____ **Room #:**_____ **A.M./P.M.** (circle one) **Date:**_____

Child's Name	Student Work Sample					Student's Oral Language				
	1	2	3	4	5	1	2	3	4	5
1.										
2.										
3.										
4.										
5.										
6.										
7.										
8.										
9.										
10.										
11.										
12.										
13.										
14.										
15.										
16.										
17.										
18.										
19.										
20.										

* Classroom Summary Sheet is to be completed and placed in the principal's mailbox no later than _____.
Adapted from Cartwright Preschool, Phoenix, Arizona, 2003.

Appendix F

Monitoring Notes Form

Name: _____ Date: _____

Activity/Center: _____

Current Student Work Level: _____

Current Oral Language Level: _____

Notes

Student:

Teacher:

Next Step:

References

Clay, Marie M. 1991. *Becoming Literate: The Construction of Inner Control.* Portsmouth, NH: Heinemann.

Clay, Marie M. 1998. *By Different Paths to Common Outcomes.* York, ME: Stenhouse Publishers.

Duncan, Marilyn. 2005. *The Kindergarten Book: A Guide to Literacy Instruction.* Katonah, NY: Richard C. Owen Publishers, Inc.

Mooney, Margaret. 1988. *Developing Life-long Readers.* Wellington, New Zealand: Learning Media.

Mooney, Margaret E. 2003. *Books for Young Learners Teacher Resource.* Katonah, NY: Richard C. Owen Publishers, Inc.

Mooney, Margaret E. 2004a. *A Book Is a Present: Selecting Text for Intentional Teaching.* Katonah, NY: Richard C. Owen Publishers, Inc.

Mooney, Margaret E. 2004b. "Characteristics of Learners." In *Literacy Learning: Teachers as Professional Decision Makers Resource Book.* Katonah, NY: Richard C. Owen Publishers, Inc.

New Zealand Ministry of Education. 1992. *Dancing with the Pen: The Learner as a Writer.* Wellington, New Zealand: Learning Media.

New Zealand Ministry of Education. 1997. *Reading for Life: The Learner as a Reader.* Wellington, New Zealand: Learning Media.

Neuman, Susan B., Carol Copple, and Sue Bredekamp. 2000. *Learning to Read and Write: Developmentally Appropriate Practices.* Washington, DC: National Association for the Education of Young Children.

Vygotsky, Lev S. 1978. *Mind in Society.* Cambridge, MA: Harvard University Press.

Index